Just a Few Sleeps Away

A family's discovery of good and evil in the aftermath of 9/11

By Mike Nichols

Twenty-five percent of the net proceeds of every book will be donated to a 9/11-related charity of the Haberman family's choice.

First Printing, 2011

ISBN 978-1-4507-8633-1

Story Hill Press

For Andrea, and all those with her.

"She (was going) to be back on the 12th or 13th. So our thing was, to make it sound like less, I just kept telling her it was only two sleeps away. That was like our thing. Whenever one of us would go out of town, you know, be away from each other, it was 'Just a few sleeps away."

— Al Kolodzik, recalling a phone conversation he had with his fiancée, Andrea Haberman, shortly after she had arrived in New York City late on the night of Sept. 10, 2001

Part One

Chapter One

Andrea Haberman and Al Kolodzik had a little competition every weekday morning. Whoever called the other one first after 7 a.m. would win. There was no real prize. The victor simply got proof that he or she was the first to think of, and call, the other — even though most days they'd only been separated for an hour and were at jobs no more than 20 to 30 miles apart.

The morning of Sept. 11, 2001, was a little different.

The evening before, Andrea had flown from Chicago to New York on her first business trip ever. A small-town Wisconsin girl who had met Al at tiny St. Norbert College near Green Bay, and then moved to Illinois to be near him, she had never even been to the East Coast before. The truth was she didn't really want to be there then.

There were, after all, a lot of other things happening in her life. At an age when lots of people are still trying to find themselves, the 25-year-old had already found everything from a promising job to a cute house on Chicago's northwest side to the guy she was going to marry and, one day, have lots of children with. It had been just five months earlier that Al, on a weekend trip back to St. Norbert, had gotten down on a knee and proposed in a gazebo along the Fox River. He told her he wanted them to spend the rest of their lives together and asked her if she wanted the same. Andrea — who had known exactly what future she wanted but didn't know that was the day Al had chosen to mark the beginning of it — quickly said yes. All the things she had dreamed of — the job, the house, a man she loved — had come together in a way almost too blissful to be true.

Unaware that Al had already asked permission of, or at least run the idea by, everyone from her younger sister Julie to her grandmother, Therese Heun, to her parents, Gordy and Kathy, Andrea couldn't wait to share the news with her family. After eating at a favorite restaurant and spending the night in Green Bay they drove directly to Gordy and Kathy's house the following day.

The Habermans live in the Town of Farmington, about seven miles northeast of West Bend and 40 miles northwest of Milwaukee. It's about a 90-minute ride from St. Norbert, and when they arrived there was still plenty of daylight. It was a warm, sunny afternoon and there is a picture of Andrea that Gordy took that day in their yard not long after they arrived. Gordy doesn't think it's the best shot he ever took of his daughter, not even the best one he took that afternoon. But there is something in it — exuberance, shared joy as she glances at someone just outside the frame, a look on her face of slight disbelief, maybe, that life had turned out to be so good — that perfectly captured the moment. In the picture, Andrea is standing in the sun, wearing a T-shirt underneath bib overalls. Her curly brown hair flows halfway down her upper arms.

There's something beautiful and innocent in the way she is standing, and in her smile. There is also something a little unusual. Enthralled with the new engagement ring on her finger, she is holding her left hand up over her chest for everyone to see. The picture is not a close-up, though, so when you look at it now, it is not the ring that is most evident. It is Andrea herself from a distance standing there with her hand held flat and diagonal over her heart, the way a young child might when facing the flag and saying the Pledge of Allegiance. It is a picture that seemed to perfectly capture both love and a certain unspoken faith that she lived in a place in the very heart of a country where surprisingly good things happen to people who deserve them.

Little did anyone know that day just how wrong that would prove to be.

*   *   *

Andrea had many reasons to smile that day, some she had, indeed, never foreseen. It was Al who had the business degree. She had been a psychology major who ended up at Carr Futures, a futures brokerage firm in Chicago, after a headhunter told her it would be a good match. It didn't seem like it at first. She was hired onto a team that supported Richard "Rick" Ferina, the head of the company's North American branch. The job included an invaluable view of the very top of the company and how it was run, a decent salary and, most importantly, the opportunity to be in Chicago near Al. For all that, though, she didn't initially like it. She'd often call Gordy and Kathy, discouraged and sometimes in tears.

"This," she would tell them, "is just so intense."

The woman she worked for was demanding, says Al. Andrea would come home and tell him that her supervisor, instead of handing work to her, would just toss it up over her cubicle. Andrea wasn't used to that. She came from a small Wisconsin town where most people said "Please" and "Thank you." She took it personally. Al told her not to.

"She's just testing you," he told her. "But if you don't like it, don't stay there."

Andrea, though, did not walk away. She didn't just stay, she prospered. She went from being tested to being trusted; worked a lot with the brokers and the marketing people, and directly for Ferina himself. She proved her competence and was rewarded with steady salary increases. Al, in the meantime, had a very good job with a Chicago highway contractor and asphalt producer and, like Andrea, wasn't afraid to work long hours. Here they were, three years out of college, still only in their mid-twenties and making enough money the month after they were engaged to close on a 1,300 square-foot Cape Cod on Chicago's Everell Avenue, near the city's border with Park Ridge. The brick house sat on a small lot, only 37-by-115 feet, but it had two full baths and a half-bath and was across the street from a manicured stretch of green space that surrounds and links the Resurrection Medical Center and nearby Resurrection High School. It was a quiet block and convenient for both Andrea, who could take the

"L" downtown, and Al, who worked mostly on the city's North Side. They moved in, had the hardwood floors refinished, painted everything and started looking for furniture, when there was time.

Chicago was busy building roads in 2001, and Al worked 70 hours a week that summer, including a lot of Saturdays. Andrea put in at least 50 hours Monday through Friday, and spent a lot of time on the weekends in Wisconsin, planning the wedding that was scheduled for September 2002.

Choosing a place for the wedding was a no-brainer. It was to take place Sept. 28, 2002, at St. Frances Cabrini in West Bend, the church the Habermans had attended for years. Finding a place for the reception proved a little more complicated. At first, Andrea just wanted to have it in her parents' spacious backyard — where Gordy had taken her picture the day of the engagement and where she and Julie and their neighborhood friends had grown up, walking in the woods and playing capture the flag and ghost in the graveyard on moonlit nights.

It is hard to imagine a safer, more carefree place than the subdivision that abutted the woods and farm fields of semi-rural Wisconsin, where the girls had the freedom to explore and lots of friends to do it with. They were, however, never far from the Haberman house or Kathy and Gordy.

Friday nights were the rare times when neither parent was home. That was a night that Gordy worked late at his restaurant, Piper's, in Mequon, and Kathy usually stayed at her mother's house in West Allis, a Milwaukee suburb, because it was near the hair salon where she worked early on Saturday mornings. Andrea, in high school by then, and Julie, three years younger, would give the neighbor kids burritos and fish sticks and goof around until Gordy pulled into the driveway. Before he made it in the front door, all their friends would flee out the back, off the Haberman deck and out into the dark woods. Even then, though, Julie and Andrea figured Gordy knew what had been going on because, within a half an hour, the neighbor kids would be back on the deck and Gordy would be there, too, sitting and laughing and talking. Together they would enjoy the night, the outdoors and the fields that led down to a small, pristine lake known as Little Green.

The backyard was ideal for hide-and-seek. Andrea finally realized, however, that it would not be ideal for a wedding. It sloped everywhere and it would be hard to find a place for the tent. There wasn't enough room for parking. The reception would have to be elsewhere. She must have looked at 20 places before settling on the Silver Spring Country Club, in Menomonee Falls, with its large, airy ballroom and spectacular, bucolic views. Andrea loved it. She loved the way everyone could move from the inside to the outside and back again. Loved the hardwood floors, the beamed ceilings and all the windows. The place had a nice flow to it. It suited her.

Julie, who Andrea had asked to be her maid of honor, didn't go along on most of the forays in search of the reception site because she was at school. She was there, though, the first time Andrea went looking for a wedding dress, and had no small amount of trepidation. If Andrea had looked at 20 reception sites, Julie was sure she would want to look at hundreds of dresses. Her fears seemed to be confirmed when, at the first bridal shop they went to, a place in Cedarburg; Julie made a suggestion about a dress she thought might work. Andrea thought it was "ugly," and said so.

"Just try it on. C'mon," said Julie and then went and sat down with Kathy, certain it was going to be a very, very long and painful day. The door from the dressing room wasn't even half-way open 10 minutes later, though, and they were stunned, Julie and Kathy both. The dress was an A-line, simple and unadorned. It hadn't looked like much on the hanger. On Andrea, though, it was enough to induce tears. It was both elegant and beautiful, the way Julie had, secretly, always thought of her big sister.

*   *   *

Gordy Haberman hunts black bear. There are three mounted in the Haberman house. What he really wanted, though, was a grizzly. He and a friend had already booked what they thought of as the "hunt of a lifetime" in Alaska the following spring; were already training for the rigors of two weeks in the Alaskan bush. He's not a man prone to irrational fear. He'd known for a while that Andrea had been asked to start traveling periodically to New York and that, after originally being scheduled to fly out on a different week, she had switched trips with a colleague and arranged to go on Sept. 10. But he didn't know until Labor Day, Sept. 3, that she would be in the World Trade Center towers — and he did not have a good feeling.

One of his customers at Piper's had been with the Secret Service and Gordy recalled the guy once telling him how close some thought the towers had come to falling after the bombing in 1993. He was concerned enough that he called his younger sister, Shelley, who travelled a bit and had been in New York several times, and hinted that it might be nice if she went along.

"Andrea has to go to New York for business," Gordy had said. "We were thinking Auntie Shelley has been to New York. None of us has been to New York. I wonder if she would want to go with her."

It was a brief conversation that had no real significance at the time. Gordy didn't even really ask a direct question. But Shelley — who would end up traveling to New York for Andrea no less than six times in the year that followed and too many times to keep track of in the decade ahead —answered it anyway. She was undergoing intensive physical therapy for serious shoulder and rotator cuff issues, and was also preparing to go to Washington, D.C.

"Oh Gordy," she said. "I'm coming off this shoulder thing and am scheduled to go out to D.C. I don't know that I can do both."

Gordy didn't say anything about his apprehension to Andrea, although, unbeknownst to him, she was thinking the same thing. She and Al had even talked about it.

"Do you think it's safe?" Andrea had asked Al.

Back in 1993, when Andrea was still at Kewaskum High School, she had actually written about the attack on the towers in a journal for school. Her teacher, Elizabeth Rydzik Biskobing, still remembered it vividly eight years after it was written. She recalled the compassion Andrea had expressed for the victims who had been killed and her bewilderment over why anyone would have done such a thing to them.

Al grew up around tall buildings. His dad, an engineer, used to take him into the Chicago skyscrapers all the time when he was growing up.

"Oh, that place is so safe now," he assured Andrea when they talked about the World Trade Center. "They've probably got so much security there, Andrea. You don't have to worry about anything. Nothing like that is going to happen."

Still, she was apprehensive; and not just because of what had happened in 1993.

Andrea wasn't afraid to speak up for herself or tell somebody she disagreed. Still, she could be quiet to the extent that some saw her as shy. She had a contemplative, artistic side and, among strangers, a reserve that made her, at times, stand back and quietly assess things before moving ahead. She never liked to rush into something — or someplace. Whenever they walked into a bar or a restaurant, Al would invariably hold the door for her and she would, just as invariably, give him a look that let him know she didn't like it. Not because she thought it was chauvinistic. She appreciated small kindnesses. No, she didn't like it because she just didn't like to be the first one in — her role exactly on the morning of Sept. 11.

Andrea was a modest person who was "not one to put herself in the middle of a situation and that is why this whole thing is so ridiculous," said her aunt Shelley. "The quietest girl in the world ends up being the middle of the biggest event of our generation."

Ferina, Andrea's boss, had a meeting in the World Trade Center at 9 a.m. on Sept. 11, but wasn't flying out until early that Tuesday morning. In order to lay the groundwork and prepare things, Andrea was asked to fly out ahead on Monday, Sept. 10 —

alone. She was busy that day. She needed to get some work done before she went to New York and spent that Monday morning at the Carr offices in Chicago before heading back to the house on Everell Avenue for a few minutes to pick up a bag. Al, who was working not far away, snuck home and met her. The trip was only going to last a couple days, and he had just seen her that morning, but they were going to miss each other and he wanted to assure her that everything was going to be fine; tell her that a little jaunt to New York was no big deal. Remind her that he loved her and say goodbye.

It wasn't quite the parting they had envisioned. As it turned out, they weren't together at home that afternoon for more than a few minutes. She had to get to the airport. The company had sent a car for her. There was barely time to hug before Andrea had to leave to make her flight — or so they thought. After waving goodbye to Al and hurrying to O'Hare, she found that her original flight was cancelled because of weather problems. Then a second flight was cancelled and she was put on a third. It was at that point, already past the dinner hour, that Al suggested she bag it.

"Just come home," he told her over the phone. O'Hare was practically right in the neighborhood, after all. "Go in the morning."

Andrea did think about it.

"If this next one is cancelled," she said, "then I'll come home."

She had, however, already checked the new luggage she had bought for the trip. It had all her makeup in there, and everything else she would need in New York.

"Who cares?" said Al.

Andrea did. She was supposed to make sure everything was ready for Ferina; wanted to do a good job. The next flight from Chicago to New York on the night of Sept. 10 went as scheduled. And so did she — a 25-year-old woman off to New York City for the first time in her life. She wasn't thrilled with the idea, but she was doing her job and, anyway, what could there possibly be to worry about? Millions of people flew in and out of New York every year. Some 40,000 people worked in the World Trade Center each day and, except for what happened in 1993, had never had a problem.

Al worked until about 7:30 that evening, and was asleep on the couch when the phone rang at about 10 p.m. It was Andrea. She was in a room at a Marriott hotel a block or two from the World Trade Center. She was tired, a little nervous, and missed Al already. She would have much preferred to be with him back at home in Chicago. But, yes, she was there.

Lying on the couch back in the house on Everell Avenue, Al tried to comfort her. Although neither had travelled for business before, they did occasionally spend nights in different cities. When they did, they always tried to minimize the amount of time they were going to be apart by counting "sleeps." That was their "thing," as Al would put it. Some people counted hours; others counted days. They counted "sleeps." He told Andrea that he loved her, that they would soon be together again and that the moment was only a few "sleeps away." Then he hung up and, before going to bed, called Gordy at the restaurant.

Gordy, who typically worked 11- or 12-hour days, remembers it being after midnight when he got the call at Piper's – already early in the morning of Sept. 11. Al thought it was a little earlier. But they both recall vividly what Al said.

"The eagle," Al told Gordy, "has landed."

Both of them had a little chuckle over the reference to Neil Armstrong in his lunar module, finally touching down on the moon with the earth all lit up beneath him.

While his daughter went to sleep in her room in the Marriott in New York, Gordy drove home from Mequon confident that all was well. Sure of the same, Al quickly fell asleep. He had to be up early and out at his job site by 6:15 a.m.

Al had already been on the job an hour the morning of Sept. 11 when Andrea called his cell phone, winning their morning competition. It was an hour later in New York, already well past

8. She had walked the block and a half from the Marriott, and made her way to the Carr offices near the top of the World Trade Center, and had already been shown to a desk and a phone. It was a clear, sunny, beautiful day in New York. She could see the Statue of Liberty as they talked. She could see the ferries crossing the Hudson River from New Jersey. It was a crystal clear view of one of the most famous views in America.

The conversation was short, maybe three to four minutes. Andrea still didn't really want to be where she was — more than a thousand feet up in the air above New York City. She missed Al enough that she teared up a little again. She was, after all, still a 25-year-old girl from a small town in Wisconsin in love with a guy halfway across the country. She would much rather have been back in Chicago where she kept a wedding planner in her desk drawer along with a big box of cereal, hand lotion and some roses from her fiancé.

There would be plenty of time for roses, though, and for everything else.

She would see Al and her mom and dad and Julie soon enough, finish the plans for the wedding, finish fixing up the house on Everell. She'd be married at St. Frances Cabrini, and dance in the ballroom of the Silver Spring Club with the beautiful views of the fall foliage and the future. She and Al would have lots of kids who would one day run under the moonlight in her parents' backyard, the way she and Julie always had, waiting for their father to get home.

Anyway, one sleep was already down.

It was the morning of Sept. 11, 2001, and she had work to do.

She hung up happy.

Chapter Two

Tricia Perrine worked for Carr Futures on the 92nd floor of the north tower of the World Trade Center. A 29-year-old credit analyst, she traveled to Chicago occasionally, and had met Andrea Haberman a few times. They had gone out for lunch. Tricia found Andrea personable, clearly smart and just as nice. Andrea was only 25, but Tricia could see that she was headed somewhere, was going to be successful. Tricia could also see, when she stood by the cubicle in Chicago with the roses and the pictures, listening to Andrea talk, one other thing:

If there's one thing about Andrea, she always thought, *it's how much in love she is.*

Tricia didn't usually start work in New York until 9 a.m. Her boss knew Andrea had never been to the offices in the World Trade Center prior to Sept. 11, though, so he asked Tricia to show up a little earlier that morning, help show Andrea around. Get there around, say, 8:30.

Tricia gladly agreed; and intended to keep her promise.

She made it to lower Manhattan much earlier that day than she normally did. She also did something else out of the ordinary that morning: She drove her car, and ended up having a hard time finding a parking place. By the time she found a spot, according to the time-stamped parking receipt she carried with her as she walked toward the twin towers, it was already 8:39.

She knew she had to meet Andrea. She was also hungry, though, and was passing by the Amish Market on Park Place and West Broadway, practically underneath the towers. Without really thinking about it, figuring it would take just another minute or two, she impulsively darted inside.

Hustling into the market, she bought a bagel and was standing near a toaster, showing a perplexed French couple how to turn it on, when there was a massive, earth-shattering explosion.

The windows of the Amish Market were blown in.

It was 8:46 a.m.

Chapter Three

Al left the job site immediately after he talked to Andrea and brought some paperwork to an asphalt plant near O'Hare. No sooner did he get there, though, when his cell phone rang again. It was about 7:50 a.m. in Chicago – 8:50 a.m. in New York – barely half an hour since he had spoken with Andrea. He answered the call and heard a familiar voice. It was his mom, and something was wrong.

A plane, she said, had just flown into one of the two towers at the World Trade Center.

"Which one," she asked, "is Andrea in?"

A plane?

Al's first thought was that it was a Cessna or something else small. And he had no idea which tower Andrea was in, or on which floor.

"I don't know," he told his mom.

But he said he would find out. He would call Andrea. He hung up and immediately called both her cell phone and the number she had given him for the desk she was using when they had talked half an hour earlier. She didn't answer either one, not the first time and not the second. Or the third. Each time he called, the lines were either busy or just rang and rang and rang, so he called Gordy and Kathy in Wisconsin. Andrea talked to her parents every day. Maybe, if Andrea was having trouble getting through to him, she was having more success calling them.

Kathy answered.

"Mom," said Al to his future mother-in-law. "Did I wake you up?"

"No," said Kathy.

"Do you have the news on?"

She didn't.

"Turn the TV on," said Al. "A plane hit the Trade Center."

Kathy didn't believe it.

"Al, c'mon," she said. "Quit joking."

But Al was not laughing.

The TV in the Haberman's house sits in a dining area between the kitchen, where Kathy had brewed a pot of coffee, and some patio doors that lead out to the large wooded backyard where the engagement picture was taken the prior spring. Kathy turned it on. There was a picture of one of the towers with thick, black smoke coming out of the top and wafting over lower Manhattan.

Kathy ran for Gordy, who hadn't arrived home until almost 2 a.m. and was still sleeping.

"Get up!" she told him. "Al said something has happened. He can't get ahold of Andrea."

There was no footage of the actual crash, just pictures of the towers and the smoke pouring out of one of them as the morning talk show personalities switched gears and tried to find out what was happening — tried to deduce whether it was pilot error, some sort of suicide or something else.

At NBC, Bryant Gumbel was sitting at an anchor desk, giving only the barest of details.

At ABC, Charlie Gibson and Diane Sawyer, hosts of "Good Morning America," like everyone else, were trying to decipher things. A reporter on the scene was describing what everybody could already see: The north tower was aflame and fire crews were on the way. Suddenly he stopped in mid-sentence.

"Oh, my God!" he said.

"Oh, God," whispered Sawyer, barely audible. "My God . . ."

It, happened in a second, was captured live. A second plane had flown into the second tower and immediately burst into flames.

At first, even the veteran newscasters weren't sure what they had seen. It took a few seconds to register.

"That," said Gibson, "looks like a second plane has just hit. We just saw another plane coming in from the side."

Gibson sounded almost as calm as he was serious.

"So," he said, "this looks like some sort of concerted effort to attack the World Trade Center that is under way in New York."

The networks immediately re-cued footage of the plane, the second plane, smashing into the World Trade Center at more than 500 mph. They played it again and then a third time.

"We will see that scene again," said Sawyer, "to make sure we saw what we thought we saw."

They had. Everyone had. It was just past 8 a.m. Wisconsin time – 9 a.m. Eastern – and a Boeing 767 had just flown into the second tower. It was both surreal and incomprehensible. This was *intentional*. The United States was under attack — and Andrea, who had never even been in those buildings until less than an hour earlier, a girl from the Town of Farmington, was right there in the middle of it.

Gordy picked up a cup of coffee that Kathy had left on the counter in the kitchen.

What he did with it wasn't out of anger, he would say later. It was out of fear.

He threw it against the wall.

Then he, like Al, started trying to call Andrea. Kathy, in the meantime, called Julie, who was away at college. Julie had a part-time job at an Applebee's, and worked late the night of Sept. 10. She slept in the next morning, just like her dad. A very light sleeper, though, she woke up quickly when the phone rang. When she heard her mom's voice, she knew immediately something had happened.

"Julie ... " said Kathy.

"Mom," she asked, "what happened?"

Julie, too, turned on the TV, but just for a minute. She knew enough already. She got in her car and turned the radio on and headed home. As she made the 90-minute drive, she looked around and noticed something: All the other drivers on the highway were on their cell phones, talking as they wore blank expressions of disbelief.

Julie herself talked only to Andrea.

"It's OK, Andrea. It's OK. We're coming to get you. You're going to be OK," she said over and over to her big sister. She drove down the highway, pausing not at all between words, running her sentences together with a rhythm that was half-assurance, half-fear. "You're going to be OK. We're coming to get you. I love you. I'm with you. I love you. I love you. We're coming to get you. Don't be scared.

Chapter Four

Tricia Perrine didn't panic, not at first. She, like everyone else in the Amish Market ran from the front, from the direction of the blast, to the back. It was crowded and people were screaming, but she felt in control. She asked a guy who she thought looked like a stockbroker what had happened.

"A small plane hit the World Trade Center," he said.

She was calm at first. For all the hysteria unfolding around her, there was, in fact, an odd juxtaposition of the surreal with the normal. The French guy she had been helping with the toaster tried to comfort her in a way that made her think he was trying to hit on her. She called her boss, who was not in the office that morning, and left a message asking if he needed her to come in.

"If you need me to come in," she said, "let me know."

She had no compulsion to run, not then. She stayed put in the market for more than 15 minutes until it was suddenly rocked by a second explosion.

"What's happening?" she asked the same stockbroker, whose name was Richard.

"Another plane hit the World Trade Center," said Richard. Still, things didn't really fully register. Not yet 30 years old and from a small town in upstate New York, she had not lived in the city during the attack on the towers eight years earlier. Terrorism still didn't even occur to her. She was still thinking that everything had been an accident.

Oh my God, she thought to herself, *what a bad pilot-error day.*

Others, though, digested things more quickly. A woman who looked foreign was lying on the floor of the market, crying out.

"It's bin Laden!" she cried. "It's terrorism!" The name didn't register, but when she heard the word "terrorism" she realized she had to get out. Richard the stockbroker warned against it.

"You don't want to go out there," he told her. "There are bodies everywhere."

Tricia insisted.

"All right," said Richard, "we'll go. But you have to hold my hand and promise not to look down."

Emotion and instinct took over for both of them. Tricia feared she might die. The inertia that kept them in the market was replaced by the need to survive. There was a bay door in the back of the market, and they opened it. One of the first things they saw was a couple taking pictures, still acting as if they were on vacation — only the picture they were taking was of a severed hand.

Most people, by then, were starting to flee.

Michael Franks, an institutional equity salesman who had been working on the 33rd floor of the north tower when the first plane hit, had gotten out of the building through what was known as the lower concourse, one floor below the lobby entrance. The concourse was teeming with people, but everyone seemed to be going in a different direction. One woman was just running around and around in an unnaturally tight circle hysterically yelling, "We're all going to die. We're all going to die," until she slipped on the wet floor and smashed her head on the marble.

Michael, who would later move to Mequon, the same city where Gordy had his restaurant, began making his way out as firefighters went to help her. As he went, he could hear a faint tinkling noise, almost like it was hailing, but more like bells, and realized it was probably the sound of glass falling from the windows high above and shattering on the pavement. There was debris everywhere, and chaos. People ran now, Michael Franks and Tricia Perrine among them.

Like Tricia, Michael didn't initially realize the magnitude of what was happening. Out of habit, he'd carried his briefcase with him as he ran out of the north tower and was concerned that he'd left a blazer behind. He wondered if he'd be able to get back in there to get it later in the day.

Fleeing toward Albany Street, which happened to be the name of the city close to where she spent her childhood, Tricia jumped over half a body. A police officer standing on the corner told her and Richard to keep running toward the ferries, and they did. But Tricia paused long enough to look up at the towers where she had worked for years, where she was supposed to be at that very moment meeting with Andrea Haberman. There were, she knew, scores of people, co-workers and friends—good friends — already working that morning just in the Carr offices alone.

"Is that what I think it is?" she asked Richard, as she looked skyward.

It was.

People were jumping from the towers.

She didn't think about what that meant.

She somehow convinced herself, she would guess later on, that they were all landing down below on big, fluffy pillows.

Chapter Five

Al, who had driven to his parents' house in Chicago, had learned from Andrea's coworkers in downtown that the Carr offices in New York were on the 92nd floor of the north tower. He stood in front of the TV, and tried to count up from the bottom. The 92nd floor, he found, was very close to where the first plane had hit.

At 9:30, President Bush came on, promising to hunt down whoever was responsible.

If there was any lingering doubt about what was happening, that it was a deliberate attack, it evaporated 10 minutes later at 9:40, when a third plane — a Boeing 757 that had left Washington's Dulles International Airport with 64 people on board — flew into the Pentagon. Networks cut to dual screens now. On one, thick smoke poured out of the towers in New York. On the other, it poured out of the Pentagon. Reporters were saying that the planes had been hijacked. Information started to stream in about where they had flown out of that morning and where they had been headed. Every other plane in the country, in the meantime, was grounded.

Then, just before 10 a.m., the networks cut back to Manhattan. The 110-story south tower of the World Trade Center, it was being reported in disbelief, had suddenly collapsed; fell down upon itself in a conflagration that seemed to engulf most of lower Manhattan. Al, stunned, immediately called the Carr offices in Chicago again, wondering if he had the correct information about where Andrea was.

"That wasn't it, right?" he asked. That wasn't the tower Carr has offices in, right?

"No," they told him. No, the Carr offices were not in the tower that had just gone down. The Carr offices were in the other tower. They were in the north tower, the one that had been hit first; the one that was still standing.

Al hung up and stood there in the home of his parents, Allen and Denise. He watched and listened to the unfathomable.

Minutes later, at 10:03 a.m. Eastern time, a fourth plane, United Airlines Flight 93 – a Boeing 757 that had taken off from Newark with 44 people on it — crashed into a field about 80 miles outside Pittsburgh. It was immediately clear that there could be no survivors. That, incredibly, made four planes that had been hijacked that morning.

And then it happened.

There was already a gaping hole in the New York skyline where the south tower — the one that Andrea had not been in — had collapsed, an ineffable dust-filled gap in the most famous skyline in the world. Suddenly, smoke started to shoot outward from the top of the north tower and then a little lower down. On TV that morning, when the north tower started to crumble, it resembled a nuclear mushroom cloud — only everything was inverted. Instead of the cloud rising toward the sky it moved down toward the earth as the building caved in upon itself. When the cloud hit the ground, it shot outward and upward again, enveloping much of lower Manhattan and rising up and enshrouding the buildings that remained.

It was 10:28 a.m. Eastern time — the exact minute of the morning that on Feb. 2, 1976, Andrea had been born.

*   *   *

Back in Chicago, where it seemed the clock had stopped forever, it was an hour earlier. It was 9:28 a.m.

Al saw the north tower collapse. He couldn't bear to watch after that. He went out the door and, in shock, just stood there outside his parents' home. When Andrea had first moved to Chicago and was looking for a job, and interviewing at Carr, she had stayed with his parents in that same house, slept in his little sister's bedroom. Al looked around in a daze at the branches and the leaves, the plants in the yard of the house he grew up in, the flowers that were still blooming in early September.

Al is a Chicago guy, and looks and talks like one He's half-Irish and half-German and is broad and handsome, with a baby face. He talks in a direct and straightforward, often humorous manner, and salts his speech with a few expletives here and there that make him a natural for the road crews and construction guys he works with every day. But he, like Julie, was talking only to Andrea then. It was a completely calm morning, and he just stood there all alone and looked around his parents' yard and wondered if she was dead. Wondered, too, if there was a way for her to just let him know, tell him. Somehow.

He was still staring at the branches and leaves, the plants and flowers. He said to her, to Andrea, "If you're dead, you know, move that branch and tell me. Or move that flower."

"You know," he said to her, "move that if you're dead or whatever."

There was no wind that morning, none, and that's the thing, he would recall years later. It was a completely still day. Every time he talked to Andrea as he stood there, though, trying the test with a branch or flower or leaf, that branch or that flower or that leaf would move. It would move ever so slightly — every single time.

It was then, for the first time, that the realization hit him: Andrea had been killed. She was dead.

Al, however, is a logical guy. Surely a branch or a leaf or a flower cannot tell a man whether the person he loves is alive or not. And hope is certainly a lot more powerful than a breeze, a lot bigger than a tiny movement of a flower petal. Surely, too, there had to be a way to get closer to where Andrea had been, if not exactly where she was. So, uncertain what to do, he decided to make the short drive back over to the house he shared with

Andrea on Everell Avenue. He figured, he would suppose much later, that maybe he could somehow be closer to her there. Only when he got there he still wasn't sure what to do other than what he always did. Out of simple habit, and perhaps the yearning for normalcy, he checked the mail.

Inside the box, he found confirmation of the reservation Andrea had made at the Silver Spring Club for their wedding reception.

Chapter Six

Kathy did not see the towers come down on TV. But she knew that they had and asked her sister Barb — one of the many family members who had quickly converged on the house outside West Bend — if Barb thought Andrea could still be alive. Barb did not mince words. "No," she said.

That day was a surreal shriek of disbelief. At one point, Gordy recalls, Kathy collapsed in the yard. She herself later recalled being in the street out in front of the house screaming at the realization that her oldest daughter, her firstborn child, the one whom she still spoke to every day on the phone, could be gone. She told herself something else, as well. Because she had boundless faith in the child she always called Andy, a girl who was excellent at problem-solving, she told herself that Andy always found the solution.

Andy is so brilliant and bright, Kathy said to herself, *so determined, loves Al so much, that she will find a way out of there.*

And they would do everything they could to help.

Gordy and Kathy had never even heard of Tricia Perrine before, never knew Andrea was supposed to meet her — had figured Rick Ferina was there, though. It wasn't until later in the day that they found out he never made it to the towers that morning. He'd been in traffic when the planes hit. That was a very good and lucky thing for him, but it also meant, they figured back in Wisconsin, that Andrea hadn't known anyone in the tower. There wasn't anybody there to look at her and say, "Andrea, come with us," to comfort her, to hold her hand. Wherever she was, she was cut off from anyone she really knew, or who really knew her — isolated not just from anyone she loved or who loved her back, but anyone with whom she'd ever exchanged more than a greeting or, perhaps, some discussion of where to sit, what computer to use.

"I don't care what you do," Kathy told someone at Carr that day on the phone. "You get Rick over there and you tell him to look for Andrea."

"We're doing the best we can, Mrs. Haberman," came the response. "We understand."

The sad fact, though, was there was very little, if anything, they could do. It was almost impossible, for starters, to even communicate with anyone anywhere in New York. The phones were mostly down and the city itself was being shut down as well. Desperate to do something, Kathy packed a duffel bag.

"What are you doing?" Gordy asked.

"I am going to find Andrea," said Kathy. "Do you realize that she is in New York by herself. If she's been hurt, she won't know where to go. If she has amnesia ... I mean, who is going to look for her?"

"But the airports are all shut down," said Gordy. "And cars aren't even allowed in the city."

Kathy said she would take a Greyhound.

"The Brooklyn Bridge is shut down," said Gordy.

"Well," Kathy wanted to know, "can't people walk across it?"

They weren't like most people worried about loved ones that day. They didn't live in New York or anywhere near it. They didn't know anybody there, didn't have a single connection to anyone who could help, or even give them good information. They had descended into a quagmire of uncertainly and helplessness. And each of them at the Haberman house reacted in a slightly different way.

Kathy is Catholic, went to the same Catholic grade school — Mary Queen of Heaven in West Allis — that Andrea attended until she was in seventh grade and the family decided to move to Farmington. Kathy's great-uncle was Cardinal Albert Meyer, the late archbishop of Chicago and, before that, of Milwaukee. Kathy had a deeply ingrained faith. She knelt down that day in what she considered the prettiest area of their yard.

"Take care of Andrea," she implored. "Please let her be safe. Bring her home to us."

Julie was a runner. In an effort to keep her mind from spinning and doing anything other than just sitting there and waiting, she went for a run. Ran for miles. Had no idea how far. The towers fell while Julie had still been in the car, and she had felt then that Andrea was gone — just, it seemed to her, *knew*. Yet she was trying her best not to know. At the end of the run, she stopped at a friend's house and, very calmly, started having a normal conversation, making small talk.

"I have to tell you something," Julie finally said, "something about Andrea."

"What?" her friend Tracy asked.

"You know the World Trade Centers? Well, she was in one, and she's gone."

"But," she added, still not wanting to hear the words she herself had spoken, "we're going to get her."

Gordy, in the meantime, started to work. Worked on a way to find and help his oldest daughter. He realized they needed to get the word out somehow that Andrea was missing, so he talked to his brothers-in-law, who worked in computers and advertising. They arranged to release a picture to the Associated Press and television networks. Gordy went through some pictures and decided on the one of Andrea standing with her hand over her heart, taken on that engagement weekend less than five months earlier. He also tried to reach authorities in New York. He tried over and over until he was finally able to reach an FBI agent there. He told the agent about his daughter, about Andrea. He asked for help — finally.

But there was no help that day.

"Listen, Mr. Haberman," responded the FBI agent, "it's total chaos here. ... We have 32 different command centers set up. ... To look for one person ... I can't help you."

That Tuesday and Wednesday were the worst of the Habermans' lives. They felt a despair that remains not fully definable. They were repeatedly stymied in their efforts to learn much of anything: where exactly she was when the plane hit and what had happened to her, whether she was dead or alive, injured or trapped.

They did learn one thing, though. They learned that while there are unconscionably evil people in the world, there are also people they see as angels. For every terrorist who is living proof that evil can be incarnate, there is someone who is proof of just the opposite: people Gordy and Kathy consider to be angels on earth.

It was sometime between midnight and 1 a.m. on Sept. 13 when the phone rang at the house in Farmington. Gordy, who hadn't slept much, was awake and quickly picked it up. He heard a young woman on the other end. It was someone about Andrea's age — though not Andrea herself.

"Hello," said the young woman. "Is this Mr. Haberman?"

"Yes," said Gordy.

The caller said her name was Jessica Kraemer — someone Gordy had never heard of or spoken to before. She was a complete stranger calling in the middle of the night.

"I want you to know," the stranger said, "I am looking for your daughter."

Gordy didn't know what to say, and the stranger just kept talking. She said she was originally from West Bend. She had moved to New York, though, and knew what it was like to be new there and to not know anyone. This young woman on the phone, Jessica, said she had already filed a missing person report at the New York City Armory, which served as a family assistance center in the days following the attack. She had already contacted a Milwaukee TV reporter and had gotten him to e-mail Andrea's picture and vital statistics, and was planning to make copies of the picture and post them around the city. She had already started making the rounds of the hospitals to find out if there was a young woman there, maybe injured and unable to communicate, who looked like Andrea.

Gordy was flabbergasted. Here was a woman he'd never even met — a woman Andrea had never met either — calling him up out of the blue in the middle of the night, saying she would try to find Andrea.

It was like an answer to a prayer.

Chapter Seven

Jessica Kraemer thought of herself as shy. She was nervous when she called Gordy that night, unsure what to say, afraid she would say the wrong thing. She was uncertain how to explain why she was doing what she was doing.

She didn't even know Andrea Haberman.

But she felt like she did.

Jessica had first visited New York on a vacation in 1998 and knew no one. Her strongest connection to the place at that time was a guy by the name of Brendan Fearon who drove a carriage in Central Park. When she went back out the following year, it was still on a lark, although she did fax some resumes around. Her mother was so upset when Jessica got an offer to work in the call center at New York Life, and took it, that she wouldn't even talk to her at first. Jessica's mom was, of course, worried — and never more so than in the days around Sept. 11 when she'd left message after message at both Jessica's home and work, trying to make sure she was OK.

Jessica lived in Red Hook, a neighborhood of Brooklyn across the East River from the World Trade Center, and got a late start to work that day. She had taken the F Train into Manhattan and walked out of the subway at 23rd St. sometime after 9 a.m. Crowds were milling about in front of the Flatiron Building, just standing in the middle of the street and blocking traffic, staring toward the World Trade Center — where, everyone could tell from the smoke pouring out, something had happened.

Jessica learned soon enough, all of them did, that an airplane had stuck one of the towers — and then the other. Things remained relatively calm until somebody screamed that a plane had also struck the Pentagon. It was only then that others started yelling. The Empire State Building is on 33rd St. and 5th Avenue, 10 blocks from where Jessica stood. It looms over the whole area, though, and some people seemed to be afraid it might be hit next. Others were staring at the towers. Suddenly somebody turned in that direction and started shrieking. Jessica realized what the rest of the world was now seeing. The south tower was no longer standing. It had fallen to the earth. Jessica, nauseated, would later conclude she was in shock by then. Unsure what else to do, she made her way to the New York Life building, on 27th Street between Madison and Park Avenues, where she worked. She sought out her coworkers and, perhaps, some sense of normalcy. Nothing that day, though, was normal. It was surreally abnormal. Coworkers at the insurance company watched things unfold on TV and called their families. It was announced that the subways were shutting down and the buses had stopped running. The company announced it was providing free meals; people could sleep there if they wanted to. Jessica did not. She wanted to get back to Red Hook, somehow.

It was a long walk to Brooklyn but doable and, after talking to her parents back in West Bend and her grandmother, and assuring them that she was OK, she decided to make the trek. It too was surreal. Even as people were dying by the thousands that day and tens of thousands of others were in a panic, some vendors continued to sell their goods, trying to make an almighty buck even amid the tragedy. Jessica was appalled. She was also exhausted. Luckily, somewhere around Chinatown, she found the trains were running again and squeezed into one.

No one spoke or, it seemed, even breathed. When they did, when they exited the subway and came up above ground again, they were told they should be careful. Next to Jessica's stop in Brooklyn, Red Cross volunteers were handing out masks. As she walked to her apartment, she realized why. Everything, the cars and the streets, the sidewalks, was covered in a layer of gray-brown ash and soot, and it was still falling from the sky like flurries of dirty snow. When she looked up through it, she saw military jets, lines of them, side-by-side in formation, screaming across the sky toward Manhattan.

Her family back in Wisconsin knew she was OK by then, but they talked time and time again that day. It was during one of those conversations that her father called out from the background. He was watching the news and shouted something to Jessica's mother about a West Bend woman, about Jessica's age, whose picture was on TV, someone who had been on a business trip to the World Trade Center — her first visit ever. Her name was Andrea Haberman.

Jessica's mom asked if she knew her.

West Bend is a relatively small place, with about 30,000 residents, and not many more in the nearby rural areas, such as the Town of Farmington, where the Habermans lived. Jessica was slightly older than Andrea and had grown up in a house only four miles away.

But "No," Jessica told her mother. She had never met Andrea.

At first, the connection was just geographic. Jessica thought of West Bend as a little place off in a corner of the world that most people never thought about or had even heard of. More people worked in the towers everyday than lived in West Bend. She was surprised there was another West Bender in New York. It was more than that, though. Jessica knew all too well what it was like to be far from home; knew, too, how deeply concerned her own parents could be about the most mundane events. She couldn't imagine what Andrea Haberman's parents were going through that morning. She just wanted to help and comfort them — wanted, mostly, though, to comfort Andrea.

They were complete strangers to each other, but Jessica had a vision in her head of this girl lying in a hospital, broken and bruised and utterly alone. She imagined bringing her flowers and good things to eat; imagined holding her hand if she was unconscious, telling her not to be afraid.

Not long after she found out about Andrea from her mom, she also talked to her grandmother, who gave her encouragement.

"I think," she told her grandmother, "I need to go and find Andrea."

It was actually much more than a thought. She had no doubt. She did not think to herself, "Should I do this?" or, "I am not sure." She knew she needed to.

"The core of my being in those moments," she would say later, "on the 12th and 13th, was finding this young woman, telling her, 'You are not alone and I am not going to leave.'"

Jessica is not a religious person, but she felt what she would later describe as an overwhelming, "higher sort of consciousness" forcing her out her door. Forcing her to go to the Armory and file a missing person report, to hospitals where she posted flier after flier — in search of a young woman she didn't know and had never met.

She is somewhere, Jessica thought to herself, *and she is alone.*

I will stay with her 24-hours-a-day, she told herself. *Stay with her until her family gets here.*

Chapter Eight

It was the call from Jessica, this stranger in New York, that caused Gordy to say, "Let's go." They finally had a contact there, and the hope of some help. Gordy, Kathy, Julie and Al packed up Al's Tahoe on Thursday, Sept. 13, and prepared to head east.

"Mom," Al assured Kathy, "we are going out to New York to find her and I will bring her home to you."

Everyone had the same hope, and there was plenty of reassurance that things would turn out OK for Andrea. But Andrea wasn't their only concern. They were concerned for each other. Their extended families, the bevy of Andrea's aunts and uncles who had converged on the house outside West Bend, were concerned about them, too — about Gordy and Julie and Al and, especially, Kathy.

"Gordy," Kathy's brother said right before they left, "if you don't bring Andrea home, make sure to bring back Kathy."

The same thought was going through Gordy's head.

If we can't find her, Gordy thought to himself, *how are we going to get through this?*

By then, they had posters and wore T-shirts with Andrea's picture and a description: Andrea, the shirts said, was 5'9" and 135 pounds; had brown eyes and highlighted, brown hair that ran mid-length down her back. She had a birthmark on her right thigh. She was wearing a Marquis-cut diamond engagement ring, a thin, gold necklace and a sapphire diamond ring. She wore a business suit the morning of Sept. 11 that was either black or blue or gray.

"If you have any information on the whereabouts of Andrea or if you have seen Andrea," it said on the shirts, "please contact her fiancé and her parents immediately." Their phone numbers were on the shirts as well.

Al, in particular, was impatient to get there. He had packed a bag of clothes for Andrea for when they found her, and once they got on the road insisted on doing most of the driving. He went 85 to 90 miles per hour the entire way, convinced that every minute could count. At one point they had to stop for gas and Gordy, reasoning that Al was tired, insisted on getting in the drivers' seat.

"Let me drive, you're tired," he told Al in the middle of the night, so Al let him — briefly. Gordy's not a wallflower, but he wasn't going 90 the way Al had been and there was no way, as a result, that Al could sleep. Years later, Al chuckled at the memory of how he got Gordy, no shrinking violet himself, out of the drivers' seat.

"You gotta pull over, I gotta pee. I forgot to go," he told Gordy.

Then, as soon as Gordy pulled the Tahoe over, Al confessed.

"All right, get out! I'm driving! You're going too slow!"

There was still some reason for optimism at that point, they guessed. By then, they knew that the plane that hit the north tower struck above the 92nd floor, though just above. Maybe, they reasoned, Andrea could have gotten down. Maybe she really was just injured and in a hospital somewhere with no way of reaching them. Rumors and unsubstantiated reports were rampant that injured people were in hospitals all up and down the East Coast. Maybe she had a shot. Maybe they did, too, because the opposite — the possibility that Andrea was gone — was unimaginable. Andrea was young, innocent and hard-working. Her main goals were the same as Al's. They already had good jobs. All they wanted was to get married and live in the house on Everell and have lots of kids, maybe even six, Andrea had told Julie. They wanted to enjoy life and just be happy. That, in fact, was the name of Andrea's fragrance, the one she wore everyday: Happy, by Clinique. It was said to smell like spring and wedding flowers. Most of them had never even heard of al-Qaida until then, and Al was pretty sure Andrea hadn't either.

Why would al-Qaida have murdered Andrea?

Yet, along with their hopes and their t-shirts and their posters, there was something else in the car — something not all of them even knew about. In addition to Andrea's clothes, alongside the hope that still outweighed the small movements of the flowers and leaves and branches, Al had brought a few other things. He had Andrea's hairbrush because, he'd been told, he might need to supply some of her DNA. He had also stopped by the dentist's office and picked up some of her records. He, in at least that way, was starting to prepare himself for the worst.

There was, however, no way to prepare himself for what confronted them when, 13 to 14 hours after leaving Chicago, they arrived around 3 in the morning on Sept. 14. On the New Jersey side of the Holland Tunnel, they looked across the Hudson at Manhattan and the dawning enormity of what had occurred.

It was dark and raining but the skyline was aglow. Right in the middle of it was a gaping hole. The fires in the wreckage of the World Trade Center were still burning, and an enormous smoke plume was still rising and drifting up over the rubble. It was apocalyptic — and so much worse than what had been captured on TV.

Oh my God, thought Gordy. *How can this be? How could this happen?*

As disturbing as the scene was from New Jersey, it was a whole different thing in the city itself. The Holland Tunnel, which leads from New Jersey to the island known as Manhattan, was finally opening to traffic. Al, Gordy, Kathy and Julie believed they were among the first outsiders not connected to the military or rescue organizations allowed through after the towers fell. What they saw stunned them.

There was a limousine immediately in front of them as they drove out of the tunnel and into Manhattan. Soldiers with M-16s stopped it and questioned the driver. He must have hassled the soldiers, complained or said something derogatory because the next thing they saw was the limo driver being ripped out of his seat and out into the street. The soldiers, not messing around, took his trunk apart with crowbars as Gordy, Kathy, Julie and Al sat there, wearing their white T-shirts and with their posters of Andrea taped to Al's windows, and stared.

Everything smelled like burned plastic and iron and soot and metal. It was a dirty smell, thick like tar, and part of it was the stench of something rotting. The smoke wasn't just hanging over Manhattan. It was everywhere, fuming up and out of the sewers. It was as if the smoke and ash of some netherworld had made its way upward and was seeping out and contaminating everything above that had once been good. Gordy felt that they had been transported into another realm. It was sickening, overwhelming and incomprehensible. What had happened — the devastation, the vastness and the scope of it — was something that would take years to respond to and even try to understand, something that would change everything.

For them, at that moment, though, their whole world boiled down to just one thing: As Gordy would later put it, "the immensity of this atrocity was reduced in our minds to fear and anguish for Andrea."

Chapter Nine

Gordy and Kathy had always done their best to protect Andrea and Julie, make sure they were safe. That was a big part of the reason they'd moved to Farmington in the first place. When Andrea was in grade school, she and Julie had attended Mary Queen of Heaven in West Allis, an inner-ring suburb of Milwaukee that had once been the home of Allis-Chalmers, the giant agricultural equipment manufacturer. They lived in a solid, well-kept neighborhood but it wasn't far from Highway 100 – a local business and retail strip that on weekend nights attracted massive numbers of "cruisers." Gordy and Kathy had a house two streets off the highway but the strip was inundated with so many cars that the cruisers had to drive off the strip for blocks just to find a spot to turn around. Many of them ended up turning around right in front of the Habermans' house.

"They would park the cars, and the kids would get out and use the side of our house as a toilet," said Kathy. "And then one night, it was on a Saturday, Gordy was washing his car and I was in the kitchen and Julie and Andy were in the front of the house. A car stopped and called the girls over. Said, 'Come here.'"

They started to walk over before realizing something wasn't right. Julie remembers Andrea pulling her back before they turned around and ran to get Gordy, who quickly got in the car he was washing and tried to chase the guy. They also called the police, who were in no way surprised. The police had been trying to find a way to deal with the cruising and all the problems it caused for years, and said they'd been getting other reports about the same sort of thing that had happened — or almost happened — to Andrea and Julie.

"We just thought, 'You know what? We're a little bit too close to Highway 100, to the cruising, to the drugs,'" Kathy said.

It was time to move.

The house they built in the Town of Farmington was at the end of a wooded cul de sac that felt a million miles away from the city. Al, the Chicago kid, still laughs about the first time he visited and met Andrea's family during Thanksgiving of 1995. Andrea had given him directions but they weren't very good. She told him to make a turn off a local highway at a nearby "city hall." Al drove and drove, back and forth, looking for a city hall like you'd see in Chicago until finally he called Andrea and said, "What the heck, I don't see any city hall."

The so-called city hall, it turned out, was actually "a one-story, 30 by 40" town hall that looked more like what you'd call a shed in Chicago.

Not that it mattered. As they were talking on the phone, Al saw a guy with a beard driving a jeep that he knew belonged to Andrea's family. On the back, there was a bumper sticker that read, "I love animals. They're delicious."

"Hey," he told Andrea, "I think I'm behind your dad."

So he beeped at the guy with the beard and the bumper sticker near the town hall building and then pulled up next to him and said, "I'm Al. And I'm lost."

And that was how they met.

Father Jeff Haines, the priest at the Habermans' parish, St. Frances Cabrini, calls their Town of Farmington neighborhood "kind of protected" and "almost idyllic."

"We have some other parishioners who live out that way," he said. "They seem remarkably close in that neighborhood. Then they had that kind of little community in their restaurant" in Mequon and everyone looked out for each other there, too.

All that gave Father Haines the sense that Kathy and Gordy's "main mission in life" was these two girls — and now one of them was missing in a place far from Farmington.

Gordy and Kathy are, by no means, rubes from the backwater. Kathy has always continued to spend a lot of time in

West Allis, and cuts hair in nearby Hales Corners. Gordy ran a successful business in one of Wisconsin's wealthiest suburbs. Farmington, where they had lived for years by 2001, though, is no small distance from Milwaukee — and Milwaukee is a world and half away from New York. Like Andrea, neither one of them had ever even been in New York City before, let alone New York City in the chaotic aftermath of the attacks. When they arrived early on the morning of Sept. 14, they felt like country bumpkins and it was clear to others who came upon them in the days that followed that they were out of their element.

It was Al who navigated them to the Waldorf Astoria hotel after coming through the Holland Tunnel. Carr was extremely helpful and had arranged rooms for them. Kathy, Al and Julie, were exhausted and had to get some sleep. Gordy, though, couldn't. Early in the morning — he remembers it still being dark — he walked down to a meeting room Carr had set up for the families of those who were missing. He was alone in the room when three men walked in. One of them was wearing a New York Police Department jacket and the two others were clearly firefighters. They smelled like soot and dust, and looked like they'd been at the site. Gordy approached them and found out they were brothers from a large family in Inwood, the northernmost neighborhood of Manhattan, and they were missing someone as well. Their youngest brother, Damian Meehan, a trader at Carr, had been in the north tower on the 92nd floor — just like Andrea. Gordy explained he was from Wisconsin, that it was his first time in New York, talked about how it had been Andrea's first time there as well, and explained that she was missing.

"We don't know anybody, don't know anything," he said. "Could I trouble you?"

Lower Manhattan was entirely blocked off to anyone other than rescue workers, the military, police and what came to be known as "deconstruction" crews. Gordy already knew that, without help, he couldn't get anywhere close to ground zero. He asked Mike, this police officer who turned out to be a detective, to take him to the spot where the towers fell, to where Andrea had been.

What Gordy didn't know at the time was that Mike Meehan had gone to ground zero within 90 minutes of the first plane strike. Initially, Mike hadn't realized Damian was even among the missing. Like so many New York City cops and firefighters, he'd just gone to help that morning as soon as he'd heard what had happened. He didn't have very good cell phone service so it wasn't until one of his sisters was able to reach him at around noon that he realized, standing there amid the rubble, that Damian — his little brother who had a pregnant wife and a little boy at home — had not been heard from. Mike helped search for days, circling around the site looking for pockets or holes, yelling down to see if anybody was still alive and listening. He stayed there so long that they eventually had to take him to a local hospital, St. Vincent's, to have his eyes flushed out. The smoke from the fires had left him unable to see clearly.

He saw more than clearly enough in the days that followed, though. When he wasn't at the site, Mike helped out at the morgue, notifying other families that their husbands or wives or children were dead. He knew how to respond to this father from Wisconsin grasping for some way, or place, to look for his daughter and wanting to go to ground zero. Mike, a stocky guy who grew up playing Gaelic football and still looks like he could run you over without even noticing, put his hands on Gordy's shoulders, looked Gordy in the eye, and shook his head slowly from side to side.

"No," he said in a calm voice. "You don't want to go down there."

Mike has a slightly different recollection of the morning he met Gordy. He thinks he and his brothers were probably there to attend a meeting of the Carr families at a more regular time, and that there were probably other people around. Gordy's memory, though, is clear. The Meehans were the first ones in the door and it was early — a memory that dovetails precisely with how he came to think of the Meehan family in the years that followed: saviors lifting Gordy and his family up by the shoulders in the darkness where they were all alone. Flying into LaGuardia years later, Gordy would look out the window and over the landscape of the city that was still being rebuilt and express deep gratitude for the things that Mike Meehan eventually did for him and his family — indeed for Andrea. It is no wonder Gordy remembered Mike and his brothers showing up in uniform in the middle of a very long and sleepless and desperate night, protecting him just a while longer from what he would eventually see.

*   *   *

While the Carr families congregated at the Waldorf on Park Avenue, the center of activity for the friends and relatives of the missing was the Armory at Lexington Avenue and 26th Street. The Armory had been set up as a family assistance center and the Habermans and Al badly wanted to get there. First thing in the morning on the 15th, they marched down there ready to find Andrea. What they found instead, says Gordy, was utter chaos infused with palpable grief. Families were showing up from all over the place, desperate for any tidbit of news — and rarely finding any that was positive. Everywhere you turned, people were crying and distraught. Gordy remembers sitting inside the Armory in the days that would follow and having his attention drawn to an older woman sitting at a table in front of a detective. She was pounding on the detective's chest, telling him that her husband and two sons were missing.

"*Where* is my family?' she was pleading. "*Where* is my family?"

This was still only days after the attacks, when the horror and the reality was just starting to crystallize and when so many were trying not to let it. People were sobbing and breaking down all around, carrying signs asking if anyone had seen their loved ones. Posters of the missing were everywhere, a sea of faces of the lost — Andrea's among them. Outside the Armory that first morning Al and the Habermans were there, one particular poster on a newspaper box caught their eye. Gordy realized it was his daughter. It was Andrea. There she was, amid thousands and thousands of the missing and murdered.

That was the moment, he'd recall years later, that his very being splintered.

"That was when my mind fragmented, right there," he said.

"You just had to split yourself," said Gordy, "from what was going on," find a way to tamp down the emotion and "steel your reserve."

It was also the moment he thought to himself, "What will happen to all these people when it rains?"

*   *   *

The poster, startling as it was to see, was also heartening. It proved that somebody had been there on Andrea's behalf — and it had to have been the stranger who'd called out of the blue and said her name was Jessica. Jessica, it would turn out, had already circulated posters all around New York. She had already been to the Armory and reported Andrea missing, had already checked the lists of the injured and dead. And she'd already been deeply impacted.

Standing in line, checking the lists in the days previous, Jessica happened to be next to a Latino woman in her late-forties or fifties who was doing the same thing — and who had just learned that her son had been killed. As Jessica stood next to her, the woman cried out that "her baby" had shown up on the list of the dead. Screaming, she grabbed Jessica and another person nearby and pulled them so tight into her chest that Jessica couldn't breathe.

"It was in that moment," Jessica would relate later, "I could no longer feel despair, sadness, anger, nothing at all. I didn't know how to feel at all. I just simply couldn't reason with it all in that moment. I suppose I shut down." The moment impacted her deeply, "and will so for the rest of my life."

The New York Life building where Jessica worked was close to the Armory. The Habermans and Al didn't know that, though, so it was a complete coincidence that they stumbled upon it on Sept. 15.

They walked in and tried to call her — and found she was there. They stood by the security desk and waited until a thin, diminutive girl with brown hair got off the elevator, walked over, and introduced herself in the lobby of this enormous New York insurance company that was built on the premise that there is a way to plan for death, but who, like everyone else, had never planned for this. Jessica had already spent days looking for Andrea by then, visiting hospitals and the Armory, putting up posters, checking the lists – and found nothing. She wasn't sure what to say, and neither were they. So mostly, they just said. "Thank you" and, trying to deal with their emotions, exchanged numbers.

To Jessica, it was clear they were "in a different emotional place than I was" and it was hard to know how best to be of comfort. The exchange was "a little bit awkward" but the overwhelming impression of them that afternoon and later when they met for dinner was one of appreciation. The dinner — outside at a restaurant in Greenwich Village that had lost power inside — was an odd juxtaposition of overwhelming tragedy and the normal conversation that comes with getting to know a complete stranger. Gordy, again, felt the fracturing of self that was necessary to continue to eat and live and interact in normal ways, engage in civil discourse even while trying to somehow process that his daughter was missing and might well have been among the thousands murdered by terrorists.

"My daughter is missing. We have no idea where she is," said Gordy, thinking back and trying to synopsize the bifurcated drift of their conversation with Jessica, this girl they did not know. "How are you?"

Of course, the other essential, underlying question was, "*Who* are you?"

Jessica was, in some ways, like Andrea. They were only about six months apart in age. They had grown up within miles of each other. Jessica went to West Bend West High School. Andrea went to Kewaskum High School, which is also in northern Washington County. They had no connections, though, beyond those; none anyway that Jessica was ever able to discover. The bond was just the simple fact that Andrea had been out there by herself in one of biggest cities in the world when the plane flew in right over her head.

"I saw it as my immediate and sole responsibility to care for Andrea in those first few days until her family could be with her again. That's as simple as it was," said Jessica. "Even though I had watched that first tower come down, I had still believed that there would be survivors and Andrea had to be one of them."

Jessica had herself gone to the city alone, knew no one, grew to love it but never forgot how lonely a place New York can be. She had felt it herself.

"I also had some periods of just sort of loneliness, but not in an overwhelming way. It's just the way the city operates, and cities can be pretty lonely. So, I can never impress enough how much I just was motivated by the fact I didn't want her to be alone."

"I think there is a lot of tragedy and sadness in the world," she said, but one of the very saddest things "is that so many people feel alone."

For Gordy, Kathy, Julie and Al in the days after Sept. 11, New York was a welter of sights and sounds and emotions. There were manifestations everywhere of the deepest sorrow humans could know. And there was outright anger. As they searched the streets and hospitals for any small sign of Andrea, one of the few pictures Gordy took was of a message someone had spray-painted on the side of a piece of machinery: "bin LADEN," it said in oversized, red and white letters, "MUST DIE!"

Along with the anger, though, was incomprehension and bewilderment. At one point, Jessica was walking along a street with Kathy when Kathy looked up at a building and asked if that was how tall the towers were. Jessica looked up and saw a building that was only about 20 stories tall, less than a fifth the height of the massive towers, and didn't know how to respond, so she just responded with the truth.

"No," she said, "the World Trade Center towers were much, much taller than this."

There was some comfort, and not just from Jessica. After putting everyone else in a cab that Friday night, Gordy walked back to the Waldorf alone. That is a very long walk. As he made his way in the gloaming of the evening, people started filtering out of office buildings, restaurants and shops, carrying candles and singing. It was a candlelight vigil and it left Gordy numb and amazed. When he got back to the Waldorf and walked inside, there were Secret Service agents everywhere, some carrying M-16s because, he found out, President Bush was also staying there. Somebody was playing a grand piano in the background and when he looked up, there on a balcony, Lena Horne was singing. It was a surreal tableau, men with guns positioned in the lobby of this plush and historic New York hotel while the famous singer tried to give voice and solace to a stunned city — and to this father from Wisconsin who had been thrust from nowhere right into the middle of it.

*   *   *

There were things that had to be done. Gordy, Kathy and Julie contributed DNA. They checked the lists of the deceased — and did not find Andrea's number. They tried to help. Al tried to volunteer to drive a truck at the site, but was rebuffed. Gordy tried to be part of a "bucket brigade," but was dissuaded as well. Time and again, they were impeded. Kathy bought flowers for Andrea at one point and Al tried to bring them in but had to settle for giving them to a dump truck driver to take them in instead. Even Jessica, one of the few bright spots along with Mike Meehan, felt like she didn't accomplish a whole lot. After all, she would say much later, she didn't find Andrea.

Eventually, Gordy — the man who along with Kathy had spent much of their lives watching over their daughters and making sure they were safe — had a hard decision to make.

"Al did not want to go home," said Gordy later. "But I had to get my wife out of there, keep the business going."

"In retrospect," he said. "I should have stayed."

Stayed to do what, he still, 10 years later, wasn't sure. He still had no answer for that because, the truth is, there was nothing more he could do. Andrea was missing and the possibility she would not be found, that she could be gone forever, was increasingly hard to deny, even if he would not, or could not, say it out loud. He didn't even talk about the possibility, although it loomed in the silence all the way back to Wisconsin.

"That," he said, "was a long ride home."

Somewhere in Pennsylvania they stopped at a rest site. It was raining, and Gordy — full of countless questions about what had happened to his oldest daughter and why, about what he could do to find out what happened to her and how to carry forward, about how to make sure the rest of his family was able to do the same — formed another question, this one for God.

"Why," he asked God, "is it necessary to take me apart from the inside?"

He thought that he and Kathy had done all the right things as parents: never put material things first, always taught Andrea and Julie to live life honestly and work hard, taught them never to hate. "That one of them became a victim perplexes me. Put me together again," he prayed. "Give me peace."

"Where do I — where do we all — go from here?" he asked.

Chapter Ten

Eight years after Sept. 11, 2001 — after all the assumptions had been made and court battles adjudicated and refusals to believe finally overcome — it was determined that 2,975 victims were killed at the World Trade Center towers, the Pentagon and the field in western Pennsylvania. Of those, according to the Associated Press, 2,751 were killed at ground zero.[1]

When Gordy, Kathy, Julie and Al returned to Wisconsin in late September 2001, however, things were nowhere near as clear. The number of dead was nothing more than a wild guesstimate. The long, painstaking process of collecting body parts from the site and getting DNA from relatives, trying to match small fragments to lives and the people who had lived them, had just started. On the morning of Sunday, Sept. 30, the New York Times was still reporting that as many as 5,960 individuals were missing. Only about 300 Trade Center victims were confirmed dead and, of those, only 238 had been identified.[2]

Andrea Haberman was not among them.

There was too much uncertainty and disbelief for the Habermans and Al to have a funeral. Yet they felt they had to have something, some sort of memorial or acknowledgement of who Andrea was and how she had lived even if they did not know exactly how or — in their most hopeful and optimistic hours

---

[1] "Official 9/11 Death Toll Climbs By One," AP and CBS News,
http://www.cbsnews.com/stories/2008/07/10/national/main4250100.shtml
(Sept. 10, 2009)

[2] "Dead and Missing," New York Times,
http://www.nytimes.com/2001/09/30/us/dead-and-missing.html (Sept. 30, 2001)

even if — she had died. So, when they got back, they talked to Kathy's priest, Father Haines, about how to proceed. It was initially difficult for the priest to know exactly how to comfort them. He wondered to himself whether to help them grieve the loss or keep hope alive, and found that what they wanted most was just a safe setting to talk away from the growing media crush, a secure place to discuss what Gordy called this "journey" they were suddenly on. When they got back from New York, they went to St. Frances and met with the priest in a little conference room off a courtyard across from the church, which sits on a hill in a residential area south of downtown West Bend.

"It was like this great puzzle they were trying to put together, you know?" said Father Haines. "Snatches, that's all they had."

It was only after a few such meetings that they all decided to have the memorial service on Sunday, Sept. 30. The Habermans wanted to have it at St. Frances, where Andrea and Al were going to get married. They couldn't, however, because the church was being renovated. The pews had all been removed. The altar was in the basement.

"It'll be next to impossible to have the group that you're going to have," the priest told Gordy and Kathy.

"A group?" responded Kathy.

"This is going to be communitywide," he told them.

Kathy, who did not want all the attention and media coverage, had not anticipated that.

"Maybe we should just have the service and tell people afterward," she said.

"No," said the priest, who knew that a lot of people would want to express their condolences and remember Andrea, "you can't do that."

"Oh, my God!" said Kathy.

Gordy didn't relish all the media coverage either. A reporter for the local paper had been assigned to cover the story and had been persistent, staking out the house in Farmington and even walking through the yard at one point. A neighbor and good friend, Kevin Smith, finally pulled his trailer in front of the Habermans' driveway as part of an effort to shield them.

Julie was at the house one day that fall when Gordy — who handled whatever media was unavoidable — finally took a call from a television reporter who had kept calling and calling and asked the most vapid question a reporter can possibly ask.

"How do you feel? How do you feel?" the reporter kept asking him. "How do you feel?"

Finally, Gordy decided to tell her.

"Ma'am, do you have kids?" he asked.

"Yes," she said.

"When you are sitting around at dinner tonight, you pick which one you don't want to be there tomorrow," he told her, "and then tell me how you feel."

Then he hung up.

Because St. Frances was being renovated, Father Haines arranged to have the memorial service at Immaculate Conception Church of Saint Mary in the Barton neighborhood of West Bend. St. Mary's, as it is typically called, is a historic old church made of what Milwaukeeans call Cream City brick, and it was inundated that day. Dozens of flower bouquets and pictures of Andrea lined the sanctuary. By then, all sorts of people were reaching out. A scholarship fund had already been established at Kewaskum High School and people far and wide were contributing. Some 500 people, many of them wearing red, white and blue ribbons, visited the church in what some thought of as a wake without a body. About 400 people attended a Mass that followed.

There were many things Father Haines could not say that Sunday, many things, he conceded right up front that could not be known: What exactly had happened to Andrea; the "twisted and irrational" thoughts of the terrorists; why "such a bad thing would happen to a good person." Those were questions Gordy knew even then that he would relentlessly pursue, but it was not a day for answers. It was partly a day for comfort and assurance that, as their priest put it, the faith and the courage they had given her through all the years would have been her strength.

Almost everybody in the immediate family stood up and spoke, and in a different way. Gordy and Al seemed to be the furthest along in knowing that Andrea was gone. The one line that Kathy kept repeating was, "If you should not come back ..."

"Moms are amazing that way," recalled the priest. "They don't give up, especially on their kids. And if there's any shred of hope, she was going to keep it alive. I admired that."

Gordy, for his part, wanted everyone that day to "celebrate a life."

And they did.

"Andrea was defined by 9/11," he said years later. "We are defined by 9/11. But there were 25 years previous."

Gordy and Kathy, Father Haines knew, were proud of everything Andrea had accomplished as an adult. But it was also clear to the priest that "she was still that little girl in their minds. And that love, that wanting so much just to know she was all right, it was beautiful. I thought, 'What a sweet, tender kind of love that these parents still have for those girls.' I thought, 'Wow.'

The first thing those who knew Andrea invariably say is that she had a rare mind — one that from the first was built for a classroom. She was quite literally born into one since Gordy and Kathy allowed a whole class of student nurses to be there the day she was born. Later on, she won science fairs and got very good grades and never got into too much trouble.

But even when she did, Gordy chuckles, she was still pretty smart about it.

Gordy laughs about the time she got caught doing something she wasn't supposed to at Mary Queen of Heaven in West Allis. She was written up and when she got home from school, Kathy found out about it and called Gordy at work and said, "Andrea has something to tell you."

Andrea got on the phone and Gordy asked what she'd done.

"I threw a grape at someone," said Andrea.

Gordy had to cover his mouth to keep from laughing.

"Why did you throw a grape at someone?" he asked.

"Because," she said, "I knew it would not make any noise."

She wasn't, in fact, a big noisemaker. She was shy, or at least reserved in a big group. She loved to laugh, though, and could be sarcastic or goofy with you if you were close enough to her.

Nicole Lecher was Andrea's best friend from the day they met at Kewaskum High School. They were barely teenagers and often silly. Nicole took to calling Andrea "Ang" or "Anre-ra." One day, while they were shopping at a Target store near Green Bay, Nicole and another friend they were with decided to play a little joke on Andrea. They had her paged.

"Anre-ra Habernaber," announced a loud voice over the public address system, asking her to report to the front of the store. "Anre-ra Habernaber."

It was just a goofy thing that young girls completely comfortable with each other would do — but Nicole, 35 years old in 2011, sat in her apartment in West Bend one day and still laughed about it, tearfully.

"I'll never laugh like that again," said Nicole of her friendship with Andrea. "I just remember laughing all the time."

The whole family laughed. Julie still laughs about the Christmas that Kathy made a Christmas tree out of grape vines — only it didn't look like a Christmas tree so much as a weapon that was about to be launched out of the living room. Andrea and Julie called it "the missile."

Andrea had a little bit of a wild side that her parents did not know about at the time, said Nicole. She liked her music: Pearl Jam and Stone Temple Pilots. Hated Hall & Oates. They drank a little in high school and more at St. Norbert— where Andrea went to study and Nicole went on the weekends to party.

After graduating from Kewaskum, Nicole hadn't gone on to school. She took a job at Broan NuTone, a factory in nearby Hartford, and worked the third shift. Every Friday, though, when she got off in the morning, she would get in her car and drive north to De Pere, where St. Norbert was located. She would track down Andrea, get the keys to her place and go over there, sack out and wait for her friend to get home. They would spend the weekend partying and hanging out before Nicole headed back to work on Monday.

Years later, going through some of sister's things, Julie came across an "unsafe riding on vehicle" ticket given to Andrea up at St. Norbert. She shook her head, smiling and wondering about the story behind that.

Andrea almost hadn't gone to St. Norbert at all. She'd gotten into the University of Wisconsin-Madison, had been there, enrolled and even had a dorm room and a roommate lined up. Then, just weeks before the semester was about to start, St. Norbert decided she was the sort of student they wanted and came up with a scholarship that made it as economical as attending Madison. St. Norbert was much smaller, a different sort of place entirely, one that suited Andrea.

"In hindsight, it was a huge decision that would change lives," said Gordy. "She went to St. Norbert and she excelled. She got the scholarship that required her to maintain a 3.0 or above average. And she did. ... She loved St. Norbert. And that's where she met Al, and fell in love with Al."

Andrea and Al started dating Sept. 23, 1995. They met through a friend at a party and shared a mutual opinion of each other: Each initially found the other "weird," according to Al. He was 18 at the time. Andrea was 19, nine months older and one inch taller. She was also, to borrow Nicole's word, "girly." Andrea had beautiful hair and graceful, polished fingernails. She, like her mother and her sister, loved to shop.

Al made Andrea laugh and she, in turn, made Al study. She, said Al, "was the only reason I got to the library, because I was hanging out with her all the time. We'd be in the library every night, and I always say she's the one that made me graduate."

"They were just perfect for each other," Nicole said. "It was an easy relationship. There was no stress. They complemented each other."

There was so much about her that was more than 9/11. In fact, everything about her was more than 9/11. She wasn't consumed by al-Qaida, likely didn't even know much about al-Qaida.

"We didn't follow politics a lot," Al said. "Our main goal was to get a good job and be successful, get married and have kids, and enjoy life. I'd never even really heard of al-Qaida until that day. I didn't know what they were all about, or anything like that, and I don't think she did either."

Andrea was a worker, always had been. Worked at her dad's restaurant. Worked in college. Worked as soon as she could after she got out. She was consumed by her job, by Al, by the wedding she was planning, by her friends and family, and everything that was to come. No one can know if they would have stayed in Chicago, but it seems likely that would have stayed somewhere in Illinois. She and Al planned to have kids and Kathy imagined that one day she'd be a grandma and drive down there to babysit.

"You're going to learn how to come down here," Andrea would say to Kathy.

"Andrea, I don't even drive to downtown (Milwaukee)," Kathy would respond.

Kathy would have driven anywhere, of course, for Andrea.

Andrea left behind many things when she left Chicago for the last time on Sept. 10. She left a calendar on her desk that she flipped over that morning and reminded everyone of how competent and meticulous she could be. "Copy Lotus notes 10 – map of office," she'd written on it. And "Phone list!!"

She left behind her parents who still couldn't help thinking of her as their little girl. She left behind Nicole and the laughter. She left behind her grandmother, Therese, who she loved deeply and had already given a present, a plant with ivory and flowers interwoven, for her birthday that wouldn't occur until Sept. 13.

She left behind a raft of aunts and uncles and other relatives who, like Shelley, were a big part of her life. She left behind Julie, who was going to be her maid of honor.

"Andrea was kind and sweet, and she was the first person I would go to if someone was mean to me, or if I needed advice," said Julie. "She was strong and sensitive, and gave the best advice. She loved her Al, and her puppies, Molly and Morgan. She was protective, and would never let someone hurt anyone she loved. She had a special magic about her."

"She," Julie said, "was my North Star."

"There was so much more to her than September eleventh."

Nicole, to this day, misses her deeply.

"There is not a day when I do not think about her ten times a day," said Nicole almost 10 years after Andrea had died. They never argued, she said, were never jealous of each other, perhaps because they had such different interests and talents. Nicole was into sports, was an athlete; Andrea was not. Nicole says she wasn't competitive academically, not like Andrea anyway.

"The things I did not possess as a human being, she did, and vice versa," said Nicole. "She was just a good person, like a really, actually good person. Had a good heart. Honest. Would never do anything ever to hurt anybody. I remember everything being good. I do not have a bad memory of her."

Julie's sadness is over things both big and small, the loss of both a friend to laugh with and a sister with whom she would have grown old.

"I will never say, 'Hey, do you want to come over for a backyard barbecue,'" or plan a birthday party for their parents, said Julie, wistfully.

Andrea did seem to have it all worked out. She had the house, the job and the wedding dress. But her aunt Shelley, 18 years older, knows, too, that Andrea was just at the beginning, that the mid-twenties are really just the start of life. So much was ahead of her and ahead of Al.

It was Father Haines, the day of the memorial service, who articulated Al's loss.

"You," he said to Al, "gave her the most precious gift a human being can give another human being. You gave her the gift of love. A gift that can never die."

It was Al who, when they got back from New York without her, turned to Kathy before the memorial service and broke down, saying, "I don't break promises. But I guess I lied to you. I didn't bring Andrea home."

"Yes, you did," said Kathy. "She's living in you, She's living in all of us."

Chapter Eleven

Memorial services in New York were different.

Seven weeks after the attack — on Sunday, Oct. 28 — a prayer and song service was held adjacent to the site that New York Mayor Rudy Giuliani was now calling "a burial ground of very, very large proportions." Thousands of people showed up that day, including Gordy, Kathy, Julie, Al and Shelley and many of the families of other victims.

According to the Giuliani's office at the time, 4,167 people remained missing that day. Only 506 bodies had been recovered, and only 454 of those had been identified. Fewer than 300 had been found intact.

One of those was Damian Meehan, the brother of the New York City detective Gordy had met at the Waldorf in the Carr Family Room just hours after arriving in New York for the first time on Sept. 14. Damian's body was found on Oct. 1 with a group of firefighters in a stairwell, and his large family had already buried him. His remains were no longer at ground zero, and the Meehans could easily have distanced themselves from much of the anguish and the searching that consumed the vast majority of the rest of the families.

Instead, they did the opposite.

The Habermans and Al had few contacts in New York; just a handful of family members of other Carr employees who got much of their information from the same place they did. Carr had a secure Web site that family members could access for information and it was helpful, if impersonal. When a Carr employee was identified as dead, their name would change color on the Web site. Carr also assigned a contact person to Al and the Habermans, someone who had known Andrea in Chicago. In New

York, though, where they needed help the most, they had almost no one but Mike.

"We couldn't have negotiated New York. We just couldn't have done it" without Mike, said Gordy. "We didn't know where Andrea was or what we were doing. He made sense out of it."

They relied on Mike to guide them around town, take them to the medical examiner's office, tell them what they needed to know and, for a time at least, hold back what he thought they didn't.

Gordy, though, was persistent. One of the very first things he'd asked Mike when he met him at the Waldorf was if Mike would also take him down to ground zero. Mike, Gordy always remembered, had gently taken him by the shoulders and told him that was not a place he wanted to be. Even seven weeks later, on the day of the memorial service, family members of some of the victims, overwhelmed, were collapsing on the perimeter of the site as they rounded a corner on Vesey Street and were hit with the reality of it. Red Cross volunteers were taking people out of the area in wheelchairs. This was not a place many people could stand.

Still, almost seven weeks after Mike has dissuaded Gordy from getting any closer, the father from Wisconsin still had the same desire to visit the spot where Andrea had last been. This time, Mike Meehan agreed to help them.

For the first time since Sept. 11, there were no workers on the site the day of the memorial service, which took place nearby. The site itself was still closed to family members — unless you had a connection like Mike Meehan. When the service was over, Mike led Gordy, Kathy, Julie, Al and Shelley through the police barricades on the periphery and onto the ground Giuliani was calling a cemetery. Very few people other than them and some of the other Meehans went that far that day. It was the first and only time until recovery efforts ceased seven months later that there was some solitude and silence. And although they'd seen the site from a distance — the piles of rubble being watered down by huge hoses attached to boom cranes, the infamous and iconic ruins of the north tower in the background — what they felt when they actually trod there caught them off guard.

The area in the middle of ground zero would later become known as "the pit" and eventually "the tub." That was after more than 100,000 truckloads of debris had been removed. In October 2001, the subterranean levels of the World Trade Center were still so full of rubble, with dirt dumped on top, that it was referred to as "the pile." Behind the pile, stretching upward even higher than it appeared from a distance, loomed what remained of the bent exoskeleton of arches and concrete latticework of the north tower. Part of the eastern side of the tower still stood up to 20 stories tall, defiantly stretching up hundreds of feet. It was, however, the base of the southern façade, with its spired arches leaning precariously inward, that provided a fuller clue of the sheer size of the buildings before they had collapsed with thousands of people inside.

What remained was tall, to be sure, and massive in all dimensions. It was also haunting and, to some, even incongruously beautiful. The ruins of the north tower presided over and above the rubble, drawing the eye and, after that, the heart like something out of an ancient dream. Only after that did the eye migrate to the vast devastation around it: the other buildings destroyed by the blasts and falling debris, the massive steel girders tossed like tiny bits of kindling into the charred pile at the bottom.

Kindling was an apt, if inexact, description because the fires that burned on Sept. 11 were so hot they had warped steel. Oct. 28, the day of the memorial ceremony, was 47 days after the attacks. Gordy quickly realized, though, after walking out onto the site, that the fires still burned with ferocious intensity in the buried, underground levels of the World Trade Center. He knew because although the subterranean Plaza, as it was known, was entombed underneath tons of rubble and dirt, the heat from the fires below carried right to the surface and prevented anyone with thin-soled shoes from standing in the same spot for more than a few moments. It was, Gordy realized, standing there that day for the first time, moving his feet up and down on the hot earth, like a furnace underneath. That was the reason, even then, massive pipes and hoses attached to boom cranes were being used to constantly water and attempt to cool the site. Gordy and the other members of their small group could stand it — quite literally — for only so long before they had to sit down on a large beam that enabled them to lift their feet up off the ground. Others, Gordy realized, had sat there as well. Some of the construction workers had even left behind a large, detailed map of where the buildings had once stood. Gordy looked at the map and tried to imagine what had once been there, some of the largest buildings in the world, places where tens of thousands of people went to work and spent much of their lives — until they were murdered on Sept. 11th.

Gordy had never seen or felt anything like it in all his life. No one had. He felt wholly unprepared for everything that he saw. It made him sick to the very pit of his stomach. It also induced him to put his arm around Kathy and make a promise.

"I am going to find out who did this," he told her.

Chapter Twelve

The families of 9/11 victims were like the families of many other victims of accidents or murders or even more ordinary deaths. They couldn't help but wonder, "What if?"

People died in the towers because they showed up on time for work, or maybe got there earlier than they normally would for a meeting. What if they hadn't? They died because they'd decided to go in on a day they normally wouldn't or because they were on a particular floor at a particular time. Andrea died because she was on her very first business trip. Of all the days in all the years, that was the day — the very first day and the very first hour — that she had to be in Carr's New York offices. What if the meeting she was attending had been the week before or the day after? What if she'd given up on catching a flight out of Chicago when plane after plane was cancelled the day before? What if the Carr offices were just one floor lower in the tower or somewhere underneath that, places where almost everyone got out?

"Your chance was better at winning the lottery than being in New York. So that's what the odds were, and why did this have to be Andrea?" said Kathy. "She shouldn't have been going that week. She did go that week. Her flight was cancelled two times, but yet, she made it on the flight. It's just hard."

What are the odds?

At the end of October, New York officially confirmed that the odds turned out to be against her. The city issued a death certificate for Andrea on Oct. 31, 2001, and listed the cause of death as physical injuries — even though it stated on the certificate that the body had not been found.

That same week, on Friday, Nov. 2, some members of the family attended an annual Mass of Remembrance for All Souls Day, a liturgy at St. Frances during which parishioners prayed for those who had passed away in the preceding year. They were no closer to knowing specifically what had happened than they had been in the first days, though, and — despite trip after trip to New York — it was wearing on all of them.

There were a lot of bad days after 9/11, but one of the worst came that November around Al's birthday when they were all together and planning to go deer hunting, trying to pretend to carry on in the normal ways when each one of them just broke down, crying.

"Al's life was ripped out from underneath him. Kathy, she has faith. However, her life was ripped and re-ripped and re-ripped," said Gordy. "It was not until November of that year that I realized we needed help."

They decided to get counseling, something that would carry on for years. The one thing they required of a doctor, and came to appreciate greatly, was that he, too, had been in New York. Moving forward required more than counseling, though. Andrea was in New York and each of them, including Shelley, felt compelled to go back time and time again. Shelley went in September after the attacks and again in October. And, although she was reluctant, she decided to go again in November for a meeting of the Carr families.

She didn't have anything to read on the way out, so at the airport in Milwaukee she stopped and, for no particular reason, picked up a copy of Reader's Digest. Gordy has Reader's Digest issues all over his house. Their parents subscribed to the magazine for years. To Gordy, in fact, Reader's Digest was "Mom's Digest," and one of the things that, along with her great affection for Andrea and Julie, defined her.

Shelley, though, did not make a habit of reading it as an adult, didn't subscribe to it. She just wanted something to read and picked up the December 2001 edition without even looking much at it. The cover had a picture of Muhammad Ali and referenced a number of stories inside: one about "The Science of God" and "A Stunning New View." There was a story about Ali and a third about "heroes" who had "lifted a nation."

Shelley doesn't think the reference to heroes was why she picked it up, at least not consciously. Just about every magazine in America was still writing about 9/11 in those days. She bought it impulsively because it was small and portable and sort of familiar. She took it on the plane. There were stories about firefighters and the passengers on Flight 93 before it crashed into a field in Pennsylvania's Somerset County. There were little vignettes about carpenters and iron workers and doormen. And then she turned to pages 86 and 87 and looked down.

Staring back at her was a picture of Andrea; the one Gordy had taken in the backyard the day she was engaged.

The picture was on a flyer that was taped to a brick wall with numerous other flyers. It was not the only picture but it was in a spot on the page where Shelley saw it immediately. She couldn't even speak, had to nudge her husband to show him what she was staring at.

Andrea.

On the opposite page, there was a poem by Henry Scott Holland that seemed to almost be written in Andrea's voice:

> *Death is nothing at all*
> *I have only slipped away into the next room.*
> *I am I and you are you,*
> *Whatever we were to each other,*
> *that we still are.*
>
> *Call me by the old familiar name.*
> *Speak of me in the easy way*
> *which you always used.*
> *Put no difference into your tone.*
> *Wear no forced air of solemnity or sorrow.*
>
> *Laugh as we always laughed*
> *at the little jokes that we enjoyed together.*

Play, smile, think of me. Pray for me.
Let my name be ever the household word
that it always was.
Let it be spoken without an effort.
Without the ghost of a shadow upon it.

Life means all that it ever meant.
It is the same as it ever was.
There is absolute and unbroken continuity.
What is this death but a negligible accident?
Why should I be out of mind
because I am out of sight?

I am but waiting for you,
for an interval.
Somewhere very near,
Just around the corner.

All is well.

-HENRY SCOTT HOLLAND

When Shelley would read the poem years later, standing in the living room of her home, she would pause a little and shake her head in disagreement with the line about death being a "negligible" accident. Even then, she could not read the entirety of the poem without being visibly and deeply affected. At the time she first saw it, what she thought was, "Well, I guess we know we are supposed to be on this flight and going to this meeting."

They would eventually deduce from the plastic sleeve on the poster and the type of tape used that it was one Julie had attached to the outside wall of the Armory in the days immediately after 9/11. That it was reprinted in "Mom's Digest" left both Shelley and Gordy particularly touched.

"If we are only able to see through the despair and the sadness and the loneliness," Shelley thought, Andrea "is reaching out and was on the plane that day," and letting them know it.

After all, of all the magazines she could have picked up and flipped through, of all the pages she could have turned to at exactly that moment as she was heading out to New York, she'd chosen that one.

What are the odds?

Chapter 13

Gordy carries a laminated card in his wallet that identifies him as, "Gordon Greg Haberman, Family Member." Late on a Monday night in June 2011, after meeting friends at a nearby restaurant, he walked over to One Liberty Plaza, a block off ground zero, and into the lobby. He pulled the card out of his wallet, showed it to two security guards who nodded and asked him to sign in, and knew they didn't have to give him directions to where he was going.

He took the elevator up to the 20th floor of the building, a ride that takes exactly 18 seconds.

"It has always bothered me that it takes only 18 seconds to go 20 floors," he said, "and Andrea was trapped for an hour and a half."

At the end of the hallway, there was a small sign that read, "Family Room." Gordy turned left, opened the door and was immediately surrounded by thousands and thousands of pictures of vibrant, smiling faces: men and women, old and young, of all ethnicities, many of them celebrating some long forgotten event, some just waiting patiently for a photographer to snap a portrait. The Family Room was where the families of the missing gathered in the first days after 9/11, and waited and grieved and prayed. It, too, is a place that has in the years since become a powerful shrine and memorial to the lost. Beside the pictures, there are flags and flowers, notes of remembrance and promise, dolls and little personal mementos and even beer cans — all the accoutrements of mourning and remembering, the meaningful and occasionally mundane things that have taken on everlasting significance.

At one time, the families could look out the windows all along one wall of the room while they waited, and see ground zero, where firefighters, construction workers and police worked to recover what remained of the bodies of their loved ones. When it was no longer useful to look through the windows for some sign of the dead on the site, the families used the glass to post pictures. At first there were just a few, and then a few more. But the number of pictures grew and multiplied until, now, just about every inch of space is covered.

Andrea is in what Gordy calls "the children's area" of the Family Room. Her pictures are laminated shots of her with her family and with Al. There are notes, too, now fading and starting to yellow, promises never to forget.

"I purposely come" late at night, sometimes as late as 2 a.m, "to be alone," said Gordy.

He walked over to the middle of the room and sat down on a leather couch surrounded on all sides by the faces of the lost, hardly any of them very old. The victims of 9/11 were largely part of professions where people made good money and retired relatively young. Most of them do not simply look healthy or fit in the pictures. Many were physically beautiful, vibrantly so. As he sat there, Gordy motioned in the direction of one of the pictures.

"This is somebody's life," said Gordy. "Every one of these pictures. Smiling. Happy. Every one, a story. Every one, a life. Every one, a family."

On a table in front of him, a gorgeous young woman, who could have been a model for something wholesome, beamed. Her name was Judy Hazel Fernandez and she must have been around Andrea's age. There were so many other pictures all about that it was hard to know, however, if she was the one he was referring to. She, like Andrea, was just one full life amid so many others, thousands of others.

It is here, said Gordy, that "the enormity closes in."

He picked up a copy of a book of poetry written by a family member of another victim. The book, which Gordy loves, is called "Odes to the Soul of Ground Zero," by Kazusada Sumiyama. It contains a poem written three months after Sept. 11.

> *"I don't think he is alive, but*
> *I cannot believe he is dead*
> *If I shed my tears,*
> *It means I surrender to Death*
> *If I pray for him,*
> *He would start for eternity*
> *I can neither weep myself*
> *Nor perform the memorial rites*
> *For the repose of his soul*
> *Yet, no doubt, what is*
> *Passing is the time.*

The first lines perfectly capture the conundrum many families found themselves in during the fall of 2001 and spring of 2002. They were not in denial about what had happened. They realized on one level that their loved ones were, in all likelihood, dead. But, perhaps because of the way it had happened, and certainly for those whose relatives had not been found — the vast majority — it just seemed beyond belief, unreal. The quest to somehow make it real, to find answers, especially for a family from the Midwest, could be exceedingly difficult.

The Habermans had no connection to anyone in New York or Washington on Sept. 11. They were just quietly living their lives in a place that was barely even a dot on the map. But through persistence — and a willingness to ask questions — Gordy was gradually thrust into the center of 9/11 events. At one point, in July 2003, he was part of a small group of victims' families who were given the opportunity to listen to a presentation by FBI Director Robert Mueller in the agency's headquarters in Washington, D.C. The presentation was high-tech. The FBI had a big screen up there and would press buttons, making charts and words flash and dazzle. It was impressive. But Gordy, this restaurant owner from some little place in Wisconsin no one had ever heard of, stood up at the end of the presentation and said he was wondering something.

"Why can't we get answers to simple questions?" he asked the director of the FBI.

He wanted to know why federal authorities would not release the flight manifests of people who had been allowed to fly out of the country after 9/11 when air traffic was at a virtual standstill. Mueller mentioned something about the right to privacy.

What about Andrea's rights? Gordy wanted to know.

There were so many questions — but also one basic one. Americans who don't visit New York or who have never been to the World Trade Center site don't realize the physical immensity of the geography itself. Here it is, lower Manhattan, with some of the most valuable real estate in the world, and there is — even in 2011 after all the rebuilding and with One World Trade Center climbing toward the yonder — this immense, still unfathomable hole in the very heart of the greatest city in America. It got there because some people climbed on planes, took them over, and flew them into some of America's tallest and most iconic buildings. It actually worked in spectacular fashion. Really, Gordy would wonder, *how did this happen*?

Even before he got to that question, though, he had another: What exactly *did* happen? What happened to all the victims? What happened to Andrea? Seven months after 9/11, what was being done to find her?

By spring of 2002, he was doubtful that Andrea would ever be found, but was more focused than ever on making sure everyone at the site tried. Access to the site was still extremely restricted at that time, but standing in the Family Room that April, back when you could still see out the windows, Gordy got some advice from a volunteer by the name of Jerry who was familiar with how things worked, and who was who. Jerry stood next to Gordy by the windows and pointed toward the site and a trailer on it and said, "That is where you want to go."

That trailer, it turned out, belonged to a guy who would become one of Gordy's closest friends, one of the same people with whom he shared supper at O'Hara's right across the street from ground zero before walking over to the Family Room that night years later: Charlie Vitchers.

Charlie worked for Bovis Lend-Lease, the big international construction firm, and had been on the site practically nonstop since Sept. 11. Because he had a lot of experience both building and demolishing big buildings, he spent the first two or three weeks doing surveys of buildings on the perimeter to see if they were stable or not. Some of the buildings had been damaged by debris and fire. There was fear of collapse. Charlie walked every floor of probably 60 buildings in those weeks, taking pictures and documenting damage. When he was done with that, he got involved in the site itself and eventually became the general superintendent for the recovery and cleanup effort.

Charlie, who would eventually collaborate on a book called, "Nine Months at Ground Zero," vividly remembers the day he first met Gordy, Kathy and Shelley after they had walked over from the Family Room. He'd been out somewhere on the site and received a call to head back to his trailer. Some people were asking to see him — the family of one of the victims. That was more than unusual. There were thousands of family members of victims, most of them from around the New York area and he'd had no interaction with any of them, not one. The question of what a family member might think about what he did everyday had never entered Charlie's mind. He just assumed that everyone figured things were going OK. He realized quickly after walking into his trailer that that was not the case. He opened the door and there stood these people from Wisconsin, who introduced themselves and explained that they'd lost their daughter. She'd come to New York the night before the attack and was all alone, and all these months later they still didn't know what had happened to her or where she was.

It was clear to Charlie that the Habermans' daughter was dead, her remains buried in the pile, and equally clear that they needed some reassurance about the process being used to find her. So he explained how the site had had been split up into a grid of small subsections, and how every bucket of debris was being sifted and raked for remains by firefighters, police and others. When something was found, a bone or a tooth, they would use a global positioning system to record the exact spot. They'd also document the exact time and date it was found and then give it to the city medical examiner's office to see if they could match it to DNA taken from family members. A lot of remains were being found, Charlie explained, and the DNA technology was outstanding. He told Gordy and Kathy he had a good process. There was also something else he didn't tell them: Not everybody was as committed to finding all the remains on the site as he was. There was pressure to just get the place cleaned up and the debris moved to a landfill on Staten Island. There was a school of thought among some city officials that it didn't matter where people's remains were found, and that the debris could just as easily be raked and sifted there as where it had landed the morning of Sept. 11th.

Earlier that same night in June 2011 when Gordy walked over the Family Room, Charlie told Gordy and a few others who shared their table at O'Hara's what he hadn't way back in the beginning – that there was pressure from some city bureaucrats to cart debris out of the site without thoroughly examining it for remains of the dead.

"They're dead. These people, they're dead. We've got to move trucks," Charlie says he was told.

"If we would have listened to the city," said Charlie, "that job could have been cleaned up and gone in three months. But then everybody in it would have been never found or found 20 miles away."

Charlie realized through the Habermans how important it was to search and rake and document everything on the site before it was moved. Others — such as his friend, Captain Michael Banker, a liaison from the New York City Fire Department who worked with Charlie every day and also had supper at O'Hara's that night in the summer of 2011 — realized the same thing.

"I would get a call from Michael or somebody else in the fire department saying, 'Charlie, two trucks just left the site. We didn't search them,'" said Charlie "And I would get ahold of the guy at the marina, they had a whole barge operation set up over there on West Street," and were loading up the barges that would then be towed over to the landfill. "I would get the numbers of the trucks, and I would call them up and I would say, "Send them back," and they would. ... They'd come back and they would dump their load. And then we would search it."

Charlie has six kids, and at the time his oldest daughter was 22, just out of college, not yet married, not all that different from Andrea. Charlie just couldn't imagine losing her — or what Gordy and Kathy were going through. But he knew how important it was for him to help find her. After he'd explained what was happening on the site, Charlie asked Gordy and Kathy to set aside for a moment the reason they were there and just tell him about themselves. He asked them who they were and what they did before Sept. 11. The more Charlie heard, the more he felt a bond. Like Charlie, Gordy likes to hunt and fish and can be very direct. Charlie looks like a guy you wouldn't want to get into a fight with. Nobody could kick his ass. He thought the same thing about Gordy, looking at him. And yet, there Gordy was back in 2001, distraught and vulnerable, and desperate to find his daughter or some evidence of what had happened to her. It struck a deep chord for Charlie, who'd worked the site practically every day for more than seven months but hadn't thought of anyone like Gordy, anyone so much like himself.

Before 9/11, it occurred to him, he and Gordy were the same guy.

"When his daughter died, Gordy went through something I wouldn't want to feel. I would never in a million years think it could happen to me," Charlie said. And if it did, he thought, how would he have reacted? He'd probably be sitting behind bars somewhere for shooting somebody, he figured.

Charlie wanted badly to assuage the Habermans' fears that Andrea wouldn't be found. He answered all their questions that day when they first visited his trailer, and he told them that if they had any more questions or wanted access to the site again, to call him. He gave them his number, and then got up to get something. When he came back, he held a metal cross burned out of a piece of steel. He handed it to them and made them a promise: "If she's on the site, we'll find her."

Carrying that cross, Gordy, Kathy and Shelly walked from the site to nearby Saint Paul's Chapel, sat down on the curb and — thanks to this guy by the name of Charlie Vitchers whom they'd just met — felt a great sense of relief.

Charlie, though, felt something more complicated. He'd just told these people with but one wish that he'd fulfill it, he'd find their daughter. And he thought to himself, "I should never have said that."

He had just made a promise he wasn't sure he could keep.

Chapter Fourteen

It was less than a month after Gordy and Kathy met Charlie Vitchers in New York when Jack Theusch, the sheriff of Washington County, showed up at their door at 4 o'clock on the afternoon of May 13, 2002.

Julie was not home and Gordy was at Piper's preparing for the dinner crowd, so Kathy was alone when she answered. She was not at all sure, at first, why Theusch was there, had no inkling of what he'd come to tell her and didn't assume it had anything to do with Andrea. Andrea, after all, had been killed in New York and all their dealings were with authorities there. Theusch normally dealt only with local matters, so Kathy's mind didn't make any connection between her oldest daughter and the sheriff standing there on her front stoop. The sheriff, meanwhile, did not at first mention Andrea by name.

"We found your daughter," is all Kathy heard him say.

Kathy, aware that Theusch was responsible only for the county, which included the Town of Farmington, thought he was talking about Julie — and the misunderstanding was too much for her to bear. She could not stand to hear any more.

When Gordy received a call at the restaurant a few minutes later, Theusch was on the other end of the line and explained he was at the house. The sheriff told Gordy that Andrea had been found, and then he told him that Kathy was "in the yard."

"He," said Gordy later, "didn't know what to do."

It was not the only time that Gordy saw people, professionals used to dealing with horrible traumas and crimes, unprepared for the level and complexity of grief in the days and months after Sept. 11. He remembers walking with Kathy, just a few days after the attack, through the Waldorf Astoria next to a priest who had

73

come to help console the families of the Carr victims. Tears were flowing down the priest's face and he was clutching his cross near his neck, murmuring to himself over and over, "God help me ... God help me ... God help me ..."

"They were overwhelmed, certainly not in matters of faith, but at the level of grief, at the trauma, the people missing, all of it," said Gordy, sitting on the back porch and looking out into his yard years later with a packet of voluminous reports he had eventually received from the Office of Chief New York Medical Examiner regarding Andrea. Those reports indicate, among other things, that DNA analysis of bone fragments takes months and, in some instances, a year. The test results that Theusch delivered to Kathy that day in May were in regard to a piece that had been recovered at the site on March 17, almost two months earlier.

They first found Andrea, it turned out, on St. Patrick's Day.

Gordy, sitting on the back porch and smoking a cigarette, said he felt bad for Theusch, who died in 2003.

"He was a good guy," said Gordy. But he was also a guy unaware, as almost everyone in Wisconsin was, of both the trauma and the processes for informing families in New York.

In New York there was a way to handle notifications. A member of the clergy typically arrived at the homes of the families along with law enforcement to bring the news. In Wisconsin, where the Habermans were among the only ones who had lost an immediate family member, no one apparently thought about that. In fact, Theusch himself had been notified no more than 90 minutes earlier, according to a report written up that day by the Missing Person's Squad of the New York City Police Department. A New York detective, Patrick Sammon, had called the Washington County Sheriff's Department that afternoon and said that DNA analysis had been used to determine that a piece of bone recovered from the World Trade Center belonged to Andrea. Sammon had also requested that the department notify the Habermans. Gordy has always felt that Theusch, at that point, could have gone to St. Frances Cabrini and asked Father Haines to come along with him to the house.

Back then, the day after the initial notification, he called Theusch and told him what had transpired at the house could never happen again. Then he called Mike Meehan, the detective in New York, and asked for advice and help. And after that, he wrote a letter to the chief medical examiner in New York and asked that the medical examiner's office and the New York City Police Department change their procedures with respect to the Habermans if notification again became necessary.

Some 9/11 families chose, in the event multiple remains were found over time, not to be notified repeatedly. Some weren't even sure they could stand being notified the first time.

"Would it be better not to ever know?" said Shelley, Gordy's sister and Andrea's aunt. "Maybe. When you have the information, you can't just put yourself in the hypothetical of 'I don't know.' But I know too there are people in New York in deep anguish because they do not know."

Gordy, for his part, wanted to know everything, but he didn't want to find out in the same way and certainly didn't want Kathy to find out that way either.

"It is our wish," wrote Gordy, "that if in the future any remains are identified of our daughter," notification be given directly to Mike Meehan. "It is not necessary nor desired that our local sheriff in Wisconsin be notified. This notification in Wisconsin can only serve to re-open and create a potential media event ... again. We do not wish this to happen. Detective Meehan shares in our grief through his own loss and understands this request."

"For the present time," Gordy also wrote, "any remains already identified of my daughter Andrea L. Haberman are to be held by the Office of the Medical Examiner. At some point in the near future, pending notification of further remains, we will arrange for her return to our home for a proper and dignified service."

Gordy would come to be very glad he had written that letter because, over the next 10 months, Mike Meehan would have to call him time and again, and his dealings with the Office of the Medical Examiner would continue for years.

Chapter Fifteen

Of the 2,751 victims who were killed on Sept. 11 at the World Trade Center, only about 1,100 had been identified eight or nine months later when the decision was made to close down the site.

Charlie had done all he could do by then. He had worked with the firefighters and the police and the Port Authority to find as many human remains as they could; limited as best he could the inclusion of remains in the truckloads of debris dumped in the Fresh Kills Landfill that was named after an estuary on Staten Island. And so his job at ground zero was done.

Within a week of receiving the initial notification about Andrea, Gordy and Kathy received a letter from former New York Mayor Rudy Giuliani explaining that there would be closing ceremonies at ground zero that would be, in part, a "tribute to the nearly 3000 people who were sacrificed in the name of freedom."

The words, in Gordy's view, were incredibly poorly chosen. On May 21, 2002, he sent an e-mail to members of some other families that had lost relatives, and expressed his frustration.

"I read with interest the letter from the Mayor of New York that I received today," he wrote. "My first reaction was to gasp in astonishment. I cannot believe that a torturous murder, perhaps as part of the story comes out, with complicity and foreknowledge, can be termed a sacrifice of my daughter in the name of freedom. The only freedom I can ascertain for certain at this point has been the freedom granted from liability to many of the responsible parties. The outrage deepens as does the spin. These words that Andrea and all the others were sacrificed in the name of freedom are meant to ease us and perhaps allow us to believe (pretend) that there is some grander, more meaningful perspective in the horrible manner they died. Something to give us comfort when we are confronted with the manner of their deaths. I do not buy it.

"In actuality, they all went to work and were tortured and then murdered . . . hopefully before being mutilated.

"The ridiculousness of our situations is just beginning to become apparent. The word futility comes to mind.

"This does not diminish my respect for all those who have labored with sensitivity amidst this atrocity. I have met some of the finest and bravest people I will ever have the pleasure to be acquainted with on that site. They should be honored. They deserve to be honored. ...

"Sorry for the frankness of this letter. I do not mean to offend. However I do not need to be placated with the grander good of this assault on my family. And while I am not from New York, I hope that this helps all of New York to go on."

There was both a ceremony for workers scheduled at the site at the end of May and a second one that families were welcome to attend on June 2. The ceremony for the workers, widely covered in the media, began with the ringing of a fire bell at 10:28 a.m. Eastern time, which was the minute the north tower fell and also the minute Andrea had been born.

There were no words spoken that day; no speeches given. Everything that could have been said had been said already. The men and women who had toiled there for more than eight months watched in silence as an honor guard marched slowly up a ramp from the site, carrying a stretcher bearing only an American flag — a symbol of all those who had never been found — and placed it inside an ambulance. A steel beam, the last one removed from the rubble, was placed under a black shroud and set on the back of a flatbed truck. While buglers played taps and helicopters flew over the site, the flag and the beam were driven away.

The ceremony that many of the family members of victims attended was later, on June 2, a Sunday. Gordy, Kathy, Julie and

Al, who had been in New York time and time again by that point, could not make it that day, so Shelley flew out to represent everyone. She stopped and bought four bouquets of flowers that Saturday after she arrived in New York: one from Gordy, Kathy and Julie, one from Al, one from Kathy's family, and one from her and her husband. Although she was the only one able to be present, she wanted everyone to be there in some way. She put the flowers in cold water in the hotel bathtub overnight, and they were still perfect the next day when she gathered them up and took a cab from the hotel in midtown Manhattan to the site.

The ceremony that day was near a cross on the site that had been formed from beams in the rubble and had provided solace over the many months to the site workers. Although the better part of a year had passed, the tragedy seemed fresh and still unfolding. Once again, as it had been on Sept. 11, the weather was oddly perfect. She started to think New York had the best weather on the planet, an incongruity for a place that knew so much death and sadness. As Shelley stood there waiting for the ceremony to begin, she happened to notice a tall guy in casual, work clothing standing not far away, waiting as well.

"I don't know if you remember me," she said. "I'm from ..."

"... the family from Wisconsin," said Charlie, finishing her sentence.

Charlie introduced Shelley to his girlfriend, Holly, who would later become his wife, and told Shelley how special Holly had been in getting him through the long months at the site. Services were held at the cross frequently, but Charlie said he'd never attended any of them. As they talked, Shelley realized Charlie did not know about the notification just weeks earlier. So just as the service was about to start, she turned to him and said, "You know, they found her."

Charlie, who had wondered if he should even have made the promise he did to find Andrea, wasn't sure he'd heard it correctly. He asked Shelley to repeat it. Andrea had been found, she said again, repeating the words that from that point on forged a bond between not just her and Charlie on the site that day but between Charlie and Gordy for what they are certain will be the rest of their lives.

The ceremony started shortly thereafter and it wasn't until the end that Charlie had a chance to respond fully. He did so by asking her something she, years later, described as poignant and memorable.

"Do you," he said, "want to put your flowers at the bottom of the pit?"

Family members were generally not allowed in the pit, even then. But Charlie sweet-talked a few of the guards and — while Holly stayed up top — walked Shelley down the ramp to the bottom, where it was still possible to stand in the footprint of the North Tower, the one Andrea had been in when it fell. Indentations were still visible in the spots that once held the perimeter columns. Along the footprint of the edge of the tower closest to the ramp, Shelley placed the bouquets — one by one.

"Andrea, these are from your Mom and Dad and Julie," she said, laying down the first of the bouquets.

"These are from Al," she said, putting down another.

There was a third from Andrea's grandmother, Kathy's mom, and the rest of the family on that side. There was another from Shelley and her husband as well, and she spoke to her niece each time she laid one down. When she was done, she said, "Andrea, we're all here with you."

Shelley and Charlie weren't really supposed to be down there and didn't have much time, so Shelley said her goodbyes and Charlie took some pictures. Gordy, looking at pictures later, could tell that one of the bouquets was placed close to the spot in the southwest corner of the footprint where Andrea's remains were first found.

Shelley, years later, wasn't sure that in the emotion of the day she'd thanked Charlie properly for finding Andrea and all those others like her. After she was killed, there was nothing more important to them in the world than finding a part of her, some tangible proof of the life she had lived, a way, too, to piece together how exactly she had died. Charlie and his colleagues gave them what they needed and wanted most. He gave them back Andrea. And he gave them more than that. With a meticulousness that Andrea herself would have cherished and at no small cost to himself, he took apart the debris and tragedy of ground zero and gave people like Gordy a chance to piece back together not just Andrea's life but his own and those of the rest of the people he loved.

First, though, Gordy had to put part of his old life behind him.

Chapter Sixteen

Every hometown should have one — a place with good coffee, affordable sandwiches and big booths that you can slide into and keep sliding until there is enough room to fit the whole family. So it was a little sad in October 2002 when Gordy announced that you wouldn't be able to get a booth at Piper's anymore.

Gordy said at the time that he didn't want the closing "characterized as a tragedy of September 11." But the truth is that the loss of Piper's was part of the ripple effect, one of the tragic reverberations that impacted not just the family of a victim but a whole community. It was just too difficult splitting time and "thought processes," as Gordy put it, between Piper's and New York. And there was just no way to continue putting in the kind of hours he'd put in for years. Still, it was also exceedingly difficult to have to sell the restaurant.

Piper's was a rare place that had become an institution in Mequon, and not just because it had good food and a faithful clientele. Gordy hadn't just fed much of the city 20 miles north of Milwaukee; he'd employed what sometimes seemed like half its kids. In addition to his regular, longtime staff, he hired hundreds and hundreds of Homestead High School students over the years, and took an intense interest in them. He knew their grade point averages before he'd hire them; let them play whatever music they wanted to in the kitchen — but made sure to ask them to explain just what it was they could possibly like about it. Among the kids he hired were countless mentally disadvantaged boys and girls. He gave them their first job and a place to be a part of something; made the restaurant into something far more than just a business.

Sally Schroeder worked at Piper's the entire time Gordy owned it, and knows the impact 9/11 had on the family. She was working the morning of Sept. 11 when the phone rang about 8 o'clock. It was Gordy, and she immediately wondered what was wrong. He worked nights and slept in the morning; never called that early. She sensed immediately something unfamiliar in his voice.

"You know Andrea's in New York?" he asked.

Everybody knew Andrea. Both she and Julie waitressed at Piper's while in high school. Sally knew, too, that Andrea was in New York.

"Well," said Gordy, "you know she was in one of the towers..."

Sally, she would remember later, almost fell to her knees that morning. She already knew about the attack because she and the cook had the radio on in the kitchen. Through the phone now, she heard Kathy screaming in the background.

It was, Sally remembers, an incredibly emotional time. The staff wore buttons with Andrea's picture on them. They made a banner with an American flag and the words "God Bless Andrea," and hung it in the restaurant. They closed Piper's down for an hour during the National Day of Prayer and Remembrance on that Friday, Sept. 14; put a sign up, closed the doors, talked and prayed, and then reopened.

Piper's, though, could never really be opened again in quite the same way it once was.

When Gordy and Kathy came back, Sally could see, the fire was out of them. People wanted to help. Longtime customers would come and in ask how they were. They were curious and kind, but even kindness can be a manifestation of change. Things were different. The place became more subdued. Gordy and Kathy had been changed by what happened, and so had the restaurant. It is impossible to come away from something like Sept. 11, they had already found, and be the same people.

"You can hear of an atrocity and ignore it," said Gordy. "But to be involved in it changes your life" — and everything about it.

Maggie Gustafson, whose 20-year-old-son Tony was murdered in Milwaukee in 1995, says that is the first thing they tell you when you go to a meeting of Parents of Murdered Children, the Milwaukee-area group she helped start.

"You will never have your old life back," she said.

"It's kind of like having a Band-Aid on your heart and somebody keeps ripping it off. It is with me every day of my life. But it makes you who you are." And eventually, she said, there "will be a new normal."

One of the worst things to tell somebody who has lost a child to murder, she said, is, "Get on with your life." That is "a horrible one" because you never get your old life back. The other thing to avoid saying is nothing.

"It means everything in the world to people who have lost someone that others remember them," she said, even if you are clumsy about it.

Those who come closest to understanding the pain and loss are other parents who have had similar experiences. That's the reason Gordy and Kathy would eventually join Maggie's group and look forward to going as much as they looked forward to anything in the years immediately after 2001. Back in November 2001, however, they were still feeling very much alone. The grief and the fears and the questions about what had happened to Andrea were fresh and ever-present.

"We were at such a low moment, almost non-functional," said Gordy. "We were really at a low point, thinking about exactly what I have told you. Andrea's alone. Who in the hell was with her? What was going through her mind? Knowing that she would have been calling out for us."

Gordy — months after 9-11 by then — was still calling Andrea's cell phone, and it was still ringing. It would ring and ring, and he would listen and listen.

"I had actually called her phone after lunch hour," one day, he said, and, of course, she did not answer it. Eventually, as he always did, he hung up, left with nothing but incomprehensible, horrible questions — and a slow afternoon at the restaurant when there was time to ponder what appeared to have been Andrea's lonely death.

Then the restaurant's phone rang. Gordy picked it up. It was a woman from New Jersey. She had no idea who Gordy was, had never been to Piper's or even heard of it until just moments earlier. She'd picked Piper's name and number out of the phone book, she said, totally at random, because her boss had some clients in Mequon and wanted to do something nice for them. She wanted to buy $200 in gift certificates.

"It's the only time in the history of the restaurant this ever happened," said Gordy, who had run the place for about 20 years by then. "She wants to buy gift certificates for people in New York" who were going to send them to clients in Mequon.

"How are things out there?" said Gordy.

"Not so good," came the reply from the young woman on the other end.

"Yeah. I can't imagine being out there all the time," said Gordy.

"Oh, you've been out here?"

Gordy mentioned Andrea, who he had just a few moments ago tried to call. Andrea, he told the stranger, had been in one of the towers.

"Really?" said the woman. "Who did she work for?"

"Carr."

There was silence on the other end.

"You're kidding," the woman finally said.

Sixty-nine employees of Carr Futures died on Sept. 11, a big number that, nevertheless, represented fewer than 3 percent of the people who died in the towers that day. And, of course, there are millions of people in the New York area.

"No," said Gordy.

"My aunt was killed with Carr," said the caller. "A woman named Diane Lipari."

Gordy, years later, would still marvel at what followed. Diane Lipari, says Gordy, was "such a beautiful woman." Tricia Perrine put together a book of all the Carr employees who died on the 92nd floor, and Diane Lipari looks like somebody you would like to know, a woman probably 10 years older than Andrea with a calm smile and dark hair, and who appears successful and poised.

"Diane was truly special," said Tricia. "She didn't have kids. I could see her being the mom of everybody." She was a "very, very nice woman."

They started talking that day, Gordy and this stranger on the phone who had called out of the blue. Diane Lipari, it turned out, was not just a Carr employee and, from what he could already tell, a good person. She had been to the Carr offices in Chicago. Andrea, thought Gordy, might have known somebody.

"You can't imagine what that did to me mentally, the relief," he said.

It would turn out, as time went on, that it was far from the only time such relief came unexpectedly at a moment they needed it most.

"For almost every negative we encountered, something came through that continued our faith," he said. "Those little things kept on happening to us. Just when we were at our lowest, we would get some type of phone call from somebody. So that started with the Lipari family out in Jersey."

There was a seed of hope that might come from getting to know the Carr families, and learning about the other people who died with Andrea that day, he thought. There was also the dawning reality, however, that whatever happened, it happened in New York and not Wisconsin. And Wisconsin was where Piper's was.

For years, the restaurant had consumed Gordy. He often was more at ease there than at home because he was always afraid something was going to go wrong. That was where his mind had to be much of the time. Now, it had to be in New York. So they made a decision. In the fall of 2002, Gordy conceded the obvious.

"Sally," he said to his longtime employee, "I can't do this." He was used to working 12- and 13-hour days, putting everything he had into the restaurant, even sacrificing time with his family. He had other things to do now. He told her he was going to have to sell.

"We really had a wonderful restaurant. It had a huge impact on the community, huge," said Sally. "I mean, the week we closed, I had people coming in and they were hugging me and kissing me and crying, and it was just unbelievable. It was devastating."

The last day Piper's was open was a Sunday. They closed that day at 1 p.m. The whole staff was there, and Gordy stood up and spoke. It was, Sally would remember later, "just terrible" because of the emotion. He spoke for an hour and thanked everybody; said that he knew one of the reasons his restaurant was so successful was because of his staff. The staff all knew, though, that it was successful because of him and the way he ran it. They gave Gordy and Kathy a plaque in memory of Andrea and everyone said goodbye. It took Sally a couple hours to leave that afternoon, and when she finally walked out the door, she was in disbelief. It had, after all, been her life for 32 years.

"It was just such a family place and so many kids came through that door. It was unbelievable," she said. She would go on to work in other places but almost 10 years later said she probably hadn't gone a day without thinking about something or someone at Piper's.

Julie understood this feeling.

"Andrea and I grew up there, and many of my parents' employees were considered family, still considered family to this day. You can't duplicate a Piper's," she said. "I can't imagine how hard that was for my parents," having to sell. "They put their hearts and souls" into it and, in a way, it too "was taken from them."

They had to give it up because — like so many other things — it was part of lives that no longer existed: their old ones.

As Kathy put it, many of those who knew her before Sept. 11 wanted her "to be the same person."

"They don't get it," she said. "I'll never be that person again. How can you be?"

Part of the reason they became increasingly drawn to New York in the years that would follow was that there were so many people there who understood that. And, of course, that's where Andrea was — as well as the answers to so many of Gordy's questions about what exactly happened the day she died, and why.

Gordy Haberman at Ground Zero

Kathy and Andrea Haberman

Al Kolodzik (top), Andrea Haberman (bottom-right), and Julie Haberman (bottom-left); the day after Andrea and Al became engaged

Andrea Haberman and Al Kolodzik

Jessica Kraemer

*Charlie Vitchers; reading
names at Ground Zero*

Damian Meehan's memorial stone in the garden at Good Shepherd

Mike Meehan; Damian Meehan's older brother

*Andrea in her parents' backyard
the day after her engagement*

Andrea Haberman's memorial stone in the garden at Good Shepherd

Andrea Lyn Haberman

PART TWO

Chapter Seventeen

The call from the niece of Diane Lipari before Piper's closed was not the only "God link" that Gordy and Kathy came to believe in as they tried to digest what had happened to Andrea, and why.

In April of 2002, when the restaurant was still open and Andrea had not yet been recovered, a different call came in one day from a woman named JoEllen Wichman. JoEllen lived in the Town of Cedarburg, just six or seven miles from Piper's, but she had never been to the restaurant. Until a couple days earlier, she had never heard of Gordy or Kathy Haberman, and no one at Piper's had heard of her. In fact, the first couple times she called, she had a hard time getting whoever answered the phone to listen. Twice, as she started to explain why she was calling, someone on the other end hung up.

JoEllen was the Bread of Life director for the Salvation Army in Plymouth, a small city about half an hour north of West Bend. Like many Salvation Army workers after 9/11, she had been asked if she was willing to go to New York and work at ground zero right after the attacks. She initially said no, largely because of a fear of flying that she'd had all her life. When her boss called the following March, though, and again asked if she was interested, she surprised herself. She didn't hesitate. In her early forties at the time, she immediately said she would go. And so, at the very last point in time anyone could be expected to overcome a fear of planes, she got on one. She arrived in New York on April 18, and found a place — and people — wholly unlike those back in Wisconsin where she lived just up the hill from a covered bridge that ran over an idyllic creek. After arriving in the city, and finding her way to ground zero, she was told to report to an orientation and found herself in a whole new world. Years later, she would still remember the first words she heard in New York.

"It is your job," said the guy running the orientation, "to shut up and listen."

He didn't mean just to him. Workers on the site still sifting through the rubble were devastated that it was about to be shut down the following month, he explained. There were still many murder victims who had not yet been found. Marriages were breaking up because some of the searchers had refused to leave ground zero for any period of time to go home. Their lives had become an attempt to recover whatever small slivers or bones or personal artifacts – jewelry or purses or cell phones – had once belonged to the men and women who had been in the towers. They would use small rakes by that time to sift through piles of dirt for anything that might have once belonged to or been part of a victim. Ground zero and what remained of the buildings were more than a crime scene, after all. The whole area was a mass grave.

In addition to being told to shut up, JoEllen and the new workers were told one other thing: Don't ever remove anything — anything at all — from the site.

JoEllen was put in charge of supplies, items such as cereal, pastries, juice, coffee, eye drops and some medical provisions, at what was known as Site Three. She worked in a small makeshift building amid the ruins, where there were remnants of streets that still had an occasional manhole cover. Mostly, though, her little building was surrounded by megalithic piles of twisted steel and dirt and concrete, and what remained of the thousands of people who had died there. The families were not yet allowed on the site at that point, but there were workers who did everything from remove garbage to spray down dirt roads to sift through rubble. When they needed a place to rest or a bite to eat, they went to JoEllen.

For the longest time she knew one of those workers, an ironworker in his twenties, only as "Cheerio Man." He came in every day and every day he had to have Cheerios. The guy just loved Cheerios. If JoEllen was out of milk, he would put juice on them and eat them that way. He had to have them. Cheerio Man was not a talker. He was just an eater. Until, at the end of April, not long before the site was to be closed and it was time for JoEllen to go home, he walked up to her holding a small package. He told her not to let anyone else see it.

"From me to you, for all you did for us," said Cheerio Man to JoEllen, handing her the package.

JoEllen had no idea what it was, and was well aware of the admonition to never, ever take anything off the site, not so much as a stone. But she couldn't say no to Cheerio Man. So, with no small amount of trepidation, she accepted it. And then something else happened that caused that trepidation to grow.

While JoEllen, at the time, knew the ironworker only as Cheerio Man, some people knew her only as "Milwaukee." She wasn't really from Milwaukee, but nobody in New York knew where the Town of Cedarburg was, so "Milwaukee" was shorthand for where she came from and who she was. People would ask her what it was like in Wisconsin and had a hard time comprehending the fact it took her an hour to mow her lawn. They were largely New Yorkers and many of them didn't even have lawns like "Milwaukee" did. They were intrigued, and thankful, that she would give that up for ground zero. So it wasn't entirely surprising that, about the same time she received the mysterious package from Cheerio Man, whose real name is Rafe Greco, somebody popped up out of a manhole cover outside her makeshift building one morning to check on her.

"Hey, Milwaukee!" shouted the man who suddenly emerged from what remained of the subterranean sewers. "How ya doin?"

People don't pop out of sewers every day, but then something even more surprising began to unfold. A guy by the name of Jerry Kearney, a volunteer who worked in a building off the site but made a habit of coming over and eating in her little building, piped up after hearing she was from Milwaukee.

"Milwaukee?" said Jerry, who had helped the Habermans find Charlie Vitchers months earlier and wanted to do more, "Any chance you know where Mequon is?"

He obviously didn't know himself because he didn't pronounce it correctly. He pronounced it "MEE-quon."

"You mean Mequon?" said JoEllen, giving in the proper pronunciation.

He did.

"I have a favor to ask," he said. "I've been working with a family from Mequon and I have something I would like you to deliver to them." He didn't say what it was and added that if she didn't want to deliver it, he understood. Without being any more specific, he added that she could think about it overnight and he would come back the next day with the package, which he did. Like the package Cheerio Man had given her, it was wrapped and she had no idea what was inside. The only thing on the outside was the name of a stranger she did not know, some guy named "Gordon Haberman."

"I could send it in the mail," said Jerry. "But if you would deliver it, it would be better. I thought about it. I prayed about it. You are the right person."

All she was told was that this Gordon Haberman guy had a restaurant in Mequon and she was to give the package to him — if she agreed. So she did. Once again, she accepted a mysterious package, and almost immediately had second thoughts. Within a day, after all, "Milwaukee" had to fly home to Milwaukee, something that was scary enough. A nervous flier claiming to not know what was inside the packages people were giving her from ground zero wasn't likely to go over well with airport security in New York just months after the attacks. So she called her boss back in Wisconsin and told the story, then decided she'd better open them. Before she flew home, she unwrapped both.

Cheerio Man's package contained a thing of beauty. The ironworker, disregarding all rules, had cut a small cross out of an I-beam in the rubble of the fallen towers. It was more than just metal. The cross, the symbol of suffering and rebirth cut from the wreckage and given to her as a gesture of appreciation, was proof to JoEllen that her life had a purpose and a plan. Indeed, for her, after working in the ruins of the towers in what was really an enormous cemetery, it symbolized the whole meaning of life. She cherished it from the first.

Then she opened the package she was supposed to deliver to this man, Gordon Haberman, whom she did not know a thing about. She unwrapped it and found a plain piece of steel, rusted and unshaped, maybe 4 inches across and 6 to 8 inches long, an inch or more thick and heavy as a rock. There was a hole in the middle for some reason, maybe a spot where a bolt had once been. She had no idea what it was.

She put both packages in her suitcase, checked them at the airport and made it home to Cedarburg without incident. By then, she had learned only the basic facts about the Habermans and Andrea, and their connection to New York and ground zero. She called Piper's and started to explain that she was "JoEllen Wichman from the Salvation Army-"

Click.

She called and tried again.

Click.

Whoever had answered the phone apparently thought she was looking for a donation.

The third time she started by asking the person on the other end to please not hang up, and said she had a message for Gordon Haberman, explained that she had something to deliver to him and wanted to come to Piper's. She got a call back from Gordy himself, who invited her and her husband to the restaurant. When they arrived, Gordy ushered them into a backroom, sat them down and told his story.

Gordy is encyclopedic and not always chronological. He is rarely overtly emotional, but he is steadfastly passionate. Julie, his youngest daughter, is right about him. He sometimes seems to know everything, particularly where 9/11 is concerned. If you don't know the connections and the people and the background, it can be hard to keep up. On the way to Piper's, JoEllen thought she would simply walk into the place, shake hands, hand the package from Jerry to this Gordon Haberman, and then be on her way.

Instead, she just shut up and listened.

"We were with him for hours," she said later. "He gave us so much information about everything. I was like a deer in the headlights. Being with Gordy can be overwhelming because he knows so much about this tragedy" and it sometimes emerges from him in vast torrents that can seem like non sequiturs.

"Gordon," she said finally, sitting in the backroom at Piper's when he stopped talking and she realized all he'd been through already and all that he knew, "this is the package Jerry gave me to give to you."

Gordy opened it, explaining that he and Kathy wanted to build a memorial garden and didn't have anything of Andrea. At the time, nothing of her had been recovered and they just wanted something from the site. The amorphous piece of steel was important simply because it came from the place where Andrea had been, like the rest of steel on the site and the beautiful cross. JoEllen continued to listen. At the end, she opened her purse and took out her cross, her symbol of purpose in life and perhaps the one object that meant more to her than any other. She explained about Cheerio Man, and how he had made it from the steel that remained in the dust after the towers had fallen. And she pushed it across the table.

Gordy refused.

"I can't take this from you," said Gordy.

JoEllen insisted.

"No, I can't do this," he said.

Gordy knew where JoEllen had been on the site, and how traumatizing it could be. He knew, too, the significance and power of the steel that remained after the towers fell, and what it meant to the people who worked there — particularly a piece of steel that had been formed into a cross at a time when people were being severely tested in their faith. He wouldn't take it. He suspected what it meant to her, and was right. JoEllen remembers being at home, upon her return from New York, with the two pieces of steel in front of her: the cross, the symbol of suffering and the gift of gratitude, and the chunk of iron. She had them laid out side by side. She badly wanted Gordy to have everything he could have from the site, but tears streamed down her face as her husband watched.

"Jo," he said, "you can't give up your cross."

She felt in her heart she had to, though, and in the days after meeting Gordy at Piper's. She became intent on finding a way to get him to accept it. Then she had an idea.

The City of Milwaukee, unlike the Town of Cedarburg, is not a place where most people have lawns that take an hour to mow. But it is a hub of world-class, metal-working companies, and JoEllen's brother happened to work at one of them, Ladish.

She called her brother and asked if there was a way to split her cross in half, not into a right half and a left half or an upper half and a lower half, though. The cross was nearly an inch thick, and JoEllen's brother split it into a front and a back so there were two full crosses, each with one side that was shiny and smooth, and another that was a little rougher. The crosses were two halves of a whole that could always fit together again, each a symbol of great suffering and the bonds that people form in its midst — and only the first of many things Andrea's family would be given from the site.

This time Gordy accepted it, and would eventually come to put it in a place that would mean more to his family and the memory of Andrea than any other

Chapter Eighteen

By then, unbeknownst to Gordy and Kathy, there was something else that had already been found at the site.

The plastic evidence bag sitting on the table in the Haberman's kitchen had a date on it: March 10, 2002, the day it was recovered. It took years to sift through and catalog the debris removed from ground zero, however, so it was not until much later, on Easter Sunday 2004, that the phone rang back in the Town of Farmington. It was a police officer from New York, and she wanted them to know "some items" had been found.

"Shocked the hell out of me," said Gordy, standing by the table in the spring of 2011.

The officer didn't offer any details that Easter morning, other than to say where Gordy could pick the items up. Gordy didn't know what she was referring to until he flew out to New York shortly thereafter and, leaving Kathy at the hotel, went alone to the special property room that the New York Police Department had set up for families of victims. The property room was enormous; it was like going into a train station. There were eight different windows, several of them just for families of victim of 9/11 to register. There were counselors and members of the clergy present to help with the delivering of items and news. They ushered Gordy into a room and told him that workers at the site had recovered Andrea's clutch purse. A sergeant handed him the purse in the plastic evidence bag.

Gordy looked only briefly at the purse that day. It was relatively small but packed with Andrea's things. He gathered it up and walked back to the hotel, wondering how to get it in the room without Kathy seeing it. Outside the hotel, a homeless man was selling Clark candy bars from a box. Gordy gave him $20 in exchange for the four bars he had left, as well as the box. He took out the bars and placed the evidence bag containing his daughter's purse inside instead. And then he walked into the hotel, probably looking for all the world like a guy who just really liked milk chocolate and peanut butter.

Gordy showed Julie and Al the bag when he got back to Wisconsin, but never opened it for them. Nor did he look closely himself. He locked it in a room and didn't look at it again until years later, after having a conversation with someone at the National September 11 Memorial and Museum in New York who was interested in the purse and what it contained. Gordy realized then that he didn't even know if Andrea had left a note inside the morning she died, and he decided he should take a closer look. There was no note, but he did discover something else: a plastic ID with Andrea's name, the words, "1 WTC Visitor 92" and "Carr Futures Inc." and her picture with the lobby in the background.

Nine years after 9/11, he suddenly had what he thought of as "this terrible secret;" a picture of Andrea taken less than an hour before she died. There she was the morning of Sept. 11, wearing a dark suit and a necklace, smiling.

Gordy didn't immediately tell his family about the picture. He didn't do that until December 2010. And it wasn't until a Saturday in April 2011 that that he brought the plastic bag downstairs to the kitchen. Kathy was out of the house that morning as Gordy spread newspapers on top of a white tablecloth with little Easter eggs sewed into it. Several cute, ceramic bunnies sat upon their haunches nearby as he gently placed the plastic evidence bag from the New York Police Department on top of the newspapers.

The bag had no real color inside, just gray objects infused with the dust of the towers and all that was in them when they fell. The first object took shape only when he reached his hand inside and, from the grayness, slowly pulled out Andrea's clutch purse. He set it aside. Then, he reached back in and pulled out a set of charred keys.

"For her house, car," he said, placing them on the newspapers.

The Motorola cell phone he slowly retrieved from the bag was an older model that flipped open. It was barely recognizable, and falling apart.

"Believe it or not," he said, "that rang." After the towers fell and they could not find Andrea, Gordy called it every hour for weeks, even months. Al called it as well. They never got a message or a voice. It would just ring, and ring, and ring until one day it finally stopped.

From the bag, Gordy next pulled his daughter's eyeglasses. Then he opened the purse full of receipts and business cards and appointment reminders. Andrea had a library card from the Chicago suburb of Park Ridge, a business card for Al, a receipt for potpourri from a store in the Woodfield Mall in Schaumberg, Ill., another from Pier One, and dozens more. Most of the receipts and cards were stuck together, getting old and a little brittle. If you were careful, though, you could still gently separate them. There was a card from Cedar Creek Bridal, a place where Andrea had looked at wedding dresses, her Social Security card, two driver's licenses — one for Illinois and one for Wisconsin.

"She had about 150 bucks in her clutch purse here," said Gordy. "The city cut me a check for it. I have that upstairs. Never cashed it."

In addition to the money and a number of credit cards, Andrea's purse also contained a checkbook, and it, too, now sat on the newspapers atop the white tablecloth next to the old phone and the little packet of receipts and business cards and appointment reminders all fused together and graying — the things, said Gordy, that "remained of her life,"

After he took the call that Easter morning and went out to New York, Gordy asked where the clutch purse and all the things inside of it were found exactly.

"I did try and inquire about that," he said, suggesting he'd never gotten an exact answer. "Her body parts," he added, though, "I do know where they were found, where they were recovered from."

The deconstruction workers separated the 16 acres where the towers fell into grids, he said, and "when they recovered a body part or what they felt was a body part, they'd GPS it and they'd assign a grid number."

There was a lot that was never recovered. Andrea, for instance, had carried a yellow backpack and it was not with the things she left behind at the Marriott the morning of Sept. 11. So she likely had it with her, though no one ever found any sign of it. Nor did the Habermans ever get back any of her jewelry: her Marquis-cut diamond engagement ring, her earrings, a thin gold necklace or her sapphire diamond ring — things that would have been nice to have because they would last forever, much longer than the paper receipts and the checkbook and even the broken phone that they had tried for so long to call.

Gordy stood by the table and looked for a moment at that items laid out before him.

"I worry about the proper disposition of it," he said. "It's deteriorated since I got it back."

Then he gently placed the items back in the plastic bag and, before Kathy got home, used his hand to carefully sweep the small particles of gray matter that had fallen onto the newspapers beside the ceramic Easter bunnies back into the plastic evidence bag as well.

"Isn't that stupid? I'm worried about losing stuff," said Gordy. "That's what the air was like, all this dust."

Chapter Nineteen

Andrea carried the clutch purse into the lobby of the north tower shortly before 8 a.m. on Sept. 11. Visitors needed an ID to get up into the building, so the security guards took her picture and printed out the laminated card with her name and destination on it. She tucked the card, good for three days, into the purse.

Andrea had grown up about seven miles from West Bend, where most of the buildings were two or three stories high and didn't have elevators. To get to the upper floors of the north tower, you had to take an "express" elevator to a "sky lobby" on the 78th floor, then get off and transfer to a "local" elevator that went to the floors above that. It was like transferring between buses on the way to another side of a city, only these buses were headed straight up into the sky. The north tower, with its 110 stories, was more than 1,330 feet tall, and Carr's offices were near the top, a place lots of folks never wanted to be again after what happened in 1993.

When Andrea got off the elevator on the 92nd floor, she would have seen a glass wall that led to a reception area and a secretary sitting at a large desk in front of a burnished wooden backdrop that read "Carr Futures." It had the look, upon first entering, of a substantial and stolid place where money and people would be secure. She was scheduled to meet her New York colleague Tricia Perrine at 8:30 that morning. It was still only a little after 8, though, and Tricia was not yet there. A man by the name of Jan Demczur later told Gordy he'd been in the lobby early that day washing the glass that separated it from the hall where the elevators were located. Gordy believes he may have been the last person who would live beyond that morning to see Andrea alive as she was brought into the Carr offices.

The lobby, it turned out, was the nicest part of the floor, along with some of the offices along the outer walls where the senior managers worked. Most of the space toward the interior wasn't nearly as fancy or richly decorated — not like what you'd find in a white-stocking law firm or investment bank. Quite the opposite. The Carr offices on the 92nd floor of the north tower resembled thousands of other offices built into cavernous skyscrapers in New York. There was plenty of outside light on bright days like Sept. 11. Much of the interior, however, was illuminated by florescent lights built into drop ceilings that hung above generic cubicles full of computers, files and printers atop desks that, from a distance, all looked pretty similar. This was where many of the operations and sales people worked, where the heads of the trading desks spent their time when they weren't on the floor.

Past the Carr lobby and further into the 92nd floor, there were plenty of people around already that morning. Some of the brokers had been called in early for a meeting about their commission rates, and many others showed up early every day to get a jumpstart on their work and check in with colleagues elsewhere in the world. A "squawk box" — an open line between some of the traders in New York and London — reminded everyone that, no matter what time it was on America's East Coast, transactions were taking place all around the globe. Commodities were being traded. Money was being made. Men and women, successful and ambitious, many already quite wealthy at young ages, were starting their days. There was clearly another side to these people as well. Many had husband or wives or kids at home, parents they loved. You could tell from the pictures taped near their desks.

The name "World Trade Center" was not a misnomer. The Carr employees on the 92nd floor didn't just trade with the rest of the world, however. On a clear day, they could see much of it. Shown to her workspace near the windows on the west side of the building, Andrea would have been able, for the first time, to take in one of the world's most magnificent and dizzying views. She was likely just a little closer to the north side of the building than the south, nearly equidistant. From where she would have sat, enormous 50- or 60-story skyscrapers looked like little tenement buildings. The Statue of Liberty was in the distance and ferries were carrying commuters across the Hudson River. People and cars were barely visible without squinting. Even those who spent nearly every day, or night, there still found it mesmerizing.

Michael Rolando Richards was one of those people. Carr occupied most of the 92nd floor, but Richards had a deal with the Port Authority to use part of the south end of the space. He was an accomplished artist and sculptor who, it would turn out, seemed to have an almost preternatural intuition about him. African-American, he had a deep interest in the Tuskegee Airmen, the black World War II pilots who trained at Tuskegee Army Airfield in Alabama. His most famous sculpture, "Tar Baby vs. St. Sebastian," portrayed one of the Tuskegee pilots as the patron saint of soldiers who, perhaps apocryphally, is said to have been pierced with arrows by Mauretanian archers who had discovered he was a Christian. On a literal level, the sculpture didn't resemble either any particular airman or even St. Sebastian himself, however. It resembled Richards because the artist had made the statue by creating a cast of his own body. He didn't pierce his statue of St. Sebastian — of himself, in fact — with arrows, though. He was not a literalist. Richards had replaced the arrows with airplanes and fixed them to the statue in a way that made it appear they were attacking his body, a bit of artistic license that the Black Art Depot Today, a Web site dedicated to African-American art, later deemed "almost prophetic." It was an airplane, after all, that on Sept. 11, 2001, took Richards' life by flying into the floors directly above him. [3]

Andrea had never expressed herself in any similarly prophetic way. She was at one point in her life, however, unusually attuned to the 1993 terrorism at the tower.

---

[3] Haasim, *The Sculpture of Michael Rolando Richards,* 2010, http://blackartblog.blackartdepot.com/features/featured-ethnic-artist/michael-rolando-richards.html.

In the fall of 1993 when Andrea was just a senior in high school, her English teacher at Kewaskum High, Elizabeth Rydzik Biskobing, asked her students to write about an event in the news and how it had been dealt with by the media. Elizabeth did not suggest the 1993 bombing of the north tower as a topic. After all, by the time of the assignment that fall, the bombing was already seven months old. It had occurred Feb. 26 during the previous school year. As far as Biskobing could remember years later, only one student chose to write about it: Andrea. The other reason she would remember Andrea's choice was that Andrea had gone beyond the assignment about media treatment and included her personal disbelief about the terrorists' cruelty.

"She really threw me for a loop because she was so baffled by what happened," said Biskobing.

"I remember it because she became so emotionally involved in something larger than life for most of these kids," especially kids at a high school in semi-rural Wisconsin, some 900 miles from the World Trade Center.

Andrea told Al in her phone call to him shortly after being shown to a desk at the Carr offices the morning of Sept. 11 that she did not really want to be there; told him she would have preferred to be back home, that she missed him. But she never mentioned being fearful. She also didn't mention anything like that to Henry Schiff, a colleague in Chicago who just happened to answer the phone outside his office around 7:45 Central time that morning when Andrea checked in to let the team know she'd made it to the East Coast. There had been a big storm in New York City the previous day but, she told Henry, she'd finally made it to the Marriott at around 10 Eastern time the night before, had awakened early and made her way to the towers.

She and Henry worked as part of the small group that reported directly to Rick Ferina, the head of the North American division of what was then Carr Futures and later became part of Newedge. Andrea was in New York to provide support for Ferina. He hadn't arrived yet, she told Henry. He was stuck in traffic. She was waiting for him to arrive.

"I got in late," she told Henry. "But I'm here. Just wanted to let you know I'm in the office. I'm ready-"

There was no forewarning for the people having phone conversations with those in the towers that morning, no slightly detectable noise or subtle change in the normal order of things. For Henry Schiff on the morning of Sept. 11, 2001, there was just sudden silence. As he spoke with Andrea at precisely 46 minutes and 30 seconds past 7 a.m. Chicago time, the line went dead. Andrea, with no hint of why, was no longer on the other end. Because she was using an unfamiliar phone, Henry assumed she'd accidentally hit the wrong button and hung up. He thought she'd call right back, and didn't really think much about it.

Until she didn't.

Chapter Twenty

The first plane, a Boeing 767 with 92 people (including the hijackers) aboard, was descending ever so slightly when it flew directly into the middle of the north face of the north tower at 8:46 a.m. on what, everyone remarked later, was a beautifully clear and sunny morning. The wings were not level when it struck, so the tip of the right wing hit the 98th floor while most of the fuselage carried through floors 95 and 96.[4] The tip of the left wing struck lower. It hit the 94th floor, and may have done some direct damage as low as the ceiling on the east side of the 93rd.[5]

Everyone on the floors below heard and felt an explosion that was as deafening and powerful as it was sudden and unexpected. As far down as floor 33, Michael Franks, the institutional equity salesman, was in the middle of leaving a voicemail for somebody when he felt a "tremendous blast" that caused the building to sway back and forth.

"I had the sensation that the floor might just give way," he recalled years later, after moving to Mequon.

Farther up, Mike McQuade, an electrician from Sayresville, NJ, was very close to Andrea when the plane hit, albeit one floor lower. He had been working in the towers for three years and that morning happened to be installing fire alarms and smoke detectors on the west side of 91st floor. He was in a closet in the area below where Andrea was, showing one of the electricians

---

[4] James Glanz and Eric Lipton, *City in the Sky: The Rise and Fall of the World Trade Center* (New York: Times Books and Henry Holt and Company, 2003), 244.
[5] Jim Dwyer and Kevin Flynn, *102 Minutes* (New York: Times Books and Henry Hold and Company, 2005), 18.

who worked for him where to tie in to an electrical panel, when he felt the blast.

McQuade's first thought was that a high-voltage electrical riser that fed into one of the big substations built into the tower had somehow blown up. There was a tremendous amount of electricity and energy in those substations, enough to power the small town that the north tower was.

"If one of them went," he thought, "it would be like dynamite going off," and that's what it felt like. The reverberation was so powerful that it knocked one of his colleagues on the same floor off a ladder. The man landed so violently that, months later, he died of his injuries. To McQuade, the impact was similar to what he imagined it would be like to stand next to "two freight trains slamming together."

He had no idea at the time that a 767 had flown into the floors above him and carried through from the north side of the building most of the way to the south. Floor 91, though, like 92, had a drop ceiling, and parts of light fixtures and electrical components were immediately knocked out and dangled from the ceiling. When he turned and looked out the window, he saw flames and burning papers shooting downward. It was as if the entire universe and the normal order of things had been turned upside down.

McQuade realized quickly that whatever had happened had happened up above and that things were worse toward the north side of the building. Smoke started to appear as he and the others near him, dazed and trying to gather their wits, tried to grasp what in the world had just occurred. A door separated him from much of the rest of the floor, and when he went through it, two people were just standing there, waiting for the elevator, the way they might on any other day. It was bizarre, though, because when he looked a little beyond them, there was no longer an elevator. The elevator doors had been completely blown off. There was just an open shaft.

"Come on, get in here!" he shouted at them, trying to get them away from the shaft and the abyss.

There are all kinds of ironies of fate that saved or doomed people that morning in the towers. One of the two people standing in front of the shaft where the elevator used to be, McQuade was told later, was saved by his own absentmindedness. The man had intended to take the elevator up from below to a higher floor but, when somebody else got off on 91, he mistakenly stepped off there as well. As was the case with many others that day, tardiness saved his life.

What happened on the 91st floor was not unique. The north tower had 99 elevators, some of which had shafts that ran for hundreds and hundreds of feet up and down the building, and channeled the pressure of the blast. When the plane hit, flames shot up and down the shafts and blew off elevator doors all the way down to the lobbies and below. [6]

Years later, Gordy became good friends with an engineer, Bianca Figueroa, who worked on the fifth underground level of the north tower. That was 100 floors below where the plane hit, but even there, the elevator doors were blown out.

"When that plane hit over 1,200 feet above the fifth underground level, there was an immediate reaction in the elevator shafts that far down," said Gordy. "Jet fuel was pouring down there. Some died immediately while others made it out onto Vesey Street on fire" because of the fuel from the shafts. Others lived because Figueroa knew her way through the Trade Center's subterranean passages and led a group to safety.

Most of the elevators were immediately disabled, and in some places people were stuck inside. But another problem quickly developed as well: Smoke began to fill the 91st and 92nd floors, and not the sort that wafts harmlessly off a burning log. The smoke flowing out of the elevator shaft on 91, one floor below Andrea, was "a black, thick smoke" that smelled "almost like plastic burning," according to McQuade. To him, it looked almost like a black version of what cotton candy looks like as it is

---

[6] Jim Dwyer and Kevin Flynn, *102 Minutes* (New York: Times Books and Henry Holt and Company, 2005), 153.

spun around in a cotton candy machine. It was that thick, almost solid, and had particles of debris and ash in it. The electrician thought the smell was akin, if not to plastic, then to burning wires. He would also wonder later, when he found out what had happened, whether it was the heavy smell of jet fuel seeping down from above.

McQuade and those with him gathered as many people as they could into the vacant office they were in and initially tried to close the door, which had been bent off its frame. Briefly, they got down on the floor to avoid the suffocating smoke. They realized almost immediately, though, that they had to get out. In many parts of the towers that day, on floors where the damage was not as severe and the smoke not as thick and tangible, people had to decide whether to stay or go. They had a choice. Not on the 91st floor. The only choice there was living or dying. And it was clear that the only way to live was to leave.

McQuade and the others on the 91st floor were lucky. There were three stairwells that rose up through floors 91 and 92 of the north tower. The one that he went to was, like the other two, clogged with sheetrock that had been blasted off the walls from the stairwells above. Water was flowing through it and down the stairs like a waterfall. He knew the tower had large standpipes in the middle that carried massive amounts of water up to tanks near the top of the building, and realized one of them had to have broken. He and those with him, though, were fortunate — far more so than they could have realized at the time. They were able to crawl into the drywall and the water in the stairwell and somehow find an opening under and through the debris that had come crushing down from above.

"We had," he said later, "one little spot" to crawl though and make it off the floor and start heading down toward the ground within maybe 10 minutes of the time the plane hit. "We'd just crawled underneath" the drywall initially, he said, and after the first couple floors down the stairwell opened up. The lower floors, it turned out, were fine.

Mike McQuade didn't go all the way down, not at first. He stayed in the building and became a hero that morning, helping a group of people who were tearing off the wall of an elevator and tunneling into a bathroom on one of the lower floors where he ended up after descending from the 91st.

There was no descending, in the meantime, from the 92nd floor, at least not initially. On that floor – where Andrea had done all the right things, made it to New York when she was supposed to, showed up even earlier than she had to, set aside any apprehensions or fears because it was her nature to be conscientious — things were not fine. Things, all the evidence that Gordy would gather and sift through years later would show, were not fine at all.

Chapter Twenty-one

The "squawk box," the phone line between the Carr offices on the 92nd floor of the north tower in New York and those in London, remained open for just a few moments after the first plane hit. As a woman screamed in the background in New York, the Londoners heard a man's voice — they could not tell whose — yell out, "Oh, my God! Fucking hell!"

There was screaming in the background, as well, when Damian Meehan called his brother Eugene, a New York City firefighter, from the 92nd floor at 8:50 a.m., just minutes after the attack. Damian told Eugene that a plane had hit the tower and there was a lot of smoke coming in the vents. He was so calm, though, that Eugene assumed it was just a small plane.

Unlike Andrea, Damian was a New Yorker through and through, one of nine kids from a large Irish-Catholic family raised in Manhattan's Inwood neighborhood. Several of his older brothers had became police officers and firefighters, but Damian — the youngest of the seven boys —chose a different path. One of his brothers-in-law worked in the financial district and thought Damian, who had an aptitude for numbers and a toughness pounded into him by all those older brothers, might excel there the same way he had in other things.

Mike Meehan, eight years older, chuckled about what they did to the poor kid when he was young. It was, he said, "almost like torture." They made him run bases. They put him in the boxing ring with them. They placed him on their teams in Gaelic football, where he eventually outplayed all of them.

"He became," said Mike, "the best one out of all of us." A center forward, he was exceedingly quick and had excellent hands.

Damian didn't stay in Inwood, but he never strayed too far away either. He moved to the Bronx and eventually to New Jersey. He got married in June of 1998 and with his wife, Joann, had a little boy they named Damian Jr. By September 2001, she was pregnant again, with a little girl. Like Andrea, he appeared headed for a life of both family bliss and career success. A member of Carr's Energy Group, which focused on the world's top oil and gas companies, he was only 32.

Damian — who was probably sitting near the northwest corner of the 92nd floor, perhaps 100 feet from Andrea, when the plane hit — was one of the few Carr employees with access to a working phone that morning. When he informed Eugene there was a lot of smoke, his older brother told him to open the door, form a human chain with everyone else, hold on to each other and start to find a way down. There were some women screaming in the background, but Damian remained poised.

"I gotta go," he told his brother. "We're getting out of here."

The second plane flew into the south tower at 9:02. But even then, the group around Damian remained in control. At 9:30 a.m., a commodities broker in his late-twenties who typically sat right next to Damian picked up a call from his fiancée's sister. She could hear his voice saying "Hello," several times and he sounded calm. The call got disconnected quickly, without them being able to have a conversation, but not before she heard voices in the background speaking at normal levels and not at all in a panic. Not everyone on the floor, at the same time, was composed. At 9:13 a.m., a woman who briefly got through to her husband, a crude oil trader who was also on the north side of the floor, heard him answer, "Hello!" amid screaming. Then, there was a loud boom.

"Oh shit!" he exclaimed before the line cut out.

Neither Al nor Andrea's family heard from her that morning. Nor could they reach her, despite trying again and again. Few people had phones that worked in the towers, so it's quite possible she just didn't have access to one. Either that, Gordy and

Kathy speculate, or she was too shy to ask anybody to use theirs, or too scared, or injured.

Gordy has thought a lot over the years about whether he would have preferred to talk to her, had the chance the way some others did with their husbands or wives or children. But one of the things he asks himself is whether he could have "talked her through this." He knows families "that were talking to their kids," he said, "and they're shot." Mentally, they're "still devastated."

"While they were dying, the air was bad and they were split into two different groups," said Gordy. "From phone conversations that came out, apparently the elevators just blew in on each other" when the plane hit. "It was like a fireball came through the lobby." The fires, partly as a result of the jet fuel, blazed. At the same time, there was a lot of water, either from the broken standpipe or the sprinkler systems that would have given people a reprieve, and a chance.

Gordy thinks it likely, from how things unfolded, that everyone on the 92nd floor probably survived the initial attack. That was not the case on the floors above. In their book, "City in the Sky," James Glanz and Eric Lipton estimated that hundreds of people died when the Boeing slammed into the floors above the 92nd. Many were employees of Marsh & McLennan, which had offices from the 93rd to the 100th floors. [7]

"Visible fires began roaring through the ninety-sixth, ninety-seventh and ninety-eighth floors and they seemed especially intense on the east face of the building. Within a few minutes of the impact, people began falling from that face, often in tumbling, disjointed poses that suggested either semiconsciousness, paralyzing terror, physical injury or all three," they wrote. "Some of the doomed fell directly onto the plaza; others plunged through a temporary tentlike bandshell set up for a performance, apparently a concert."

---

[7] James Glanz and Eric Lipton, *City in the Sky: The Rise and Fall of the World Trade Center* (New York: Times Books and Henry Holt and Company, 2003), 243-248.

Exactly 2,479 people, not including the hijackers, died at the towers that morning, according to the New York medical examiner's office, including 147 on the planes and more than 400 rescue workers. Glanz and Lipton concluded there were 1,344 people in the north tower from the 92nd floor up and every single one perished. Many were still alive when the south tower collapsed at 9:59. It can't be known how many were still living when the north tower collapsed at 10:28.

Al, standing in the kitchen of the house on Everell Avenue in Chicago in late 2008, was blunt:

"It's just, I guess, the suffering that was done to her that really bothers me, and the fact that I don't know exactly what happened to her.

"What bothered me is the fact that she might have been tortured to death. The building might have fallen and she might have been alive. She might have been in a room where it was on fire. We don't think so. ... She didn't know anybody to the point where, 'Hey, Jim, How do I get down?' Or, no one was going to look at her and say, 'Andrea, come with us.' You know, she was all alone. People we talked to, it seems like everybody on that floor would have taken her under their wing, but what always haunted me was the fact that her death was so brutal. It's different falling asleep at night and not waking up. You know, being crushed to death — that's what really bothers me. That's what really bothered me for the first few months."

They all have questions. Kathy sometimes wonders why the helicopters hovering around the tower before it collapsed could not be used to rescue people, if not from the top, as happened in 1993, then by somehow swinging rescuers into the side of the building. She wonders too what Andrea experienced and witnessed.

"Did she need to look at people lying there, hurt and dying?" asks Kathy.

Or was she comforted in her final moments, and even hopeful about getting out.

Gordy would come to a firm and eventual conclusion — but only after years of investigation that extended far beyond the confines of what was once the 92nd floor.

Chapter Twenty-two

You never know, Gordy came to learn, where things are going to lead.

On Oct. 11, 2002, the same year JoEllen had the cross made by Cheerio Man split into identical halves, her phone rang early in the morning. It was Gordy. He had been watching the news. Many people — 10, it would eventually turn out — had been killed in a 38-car pileup caused by dense fog some 35 miles north of Milwaukee on I-43, near the Ozaukee-Sheboygan County line. Dozens more were severely injured. The fog was so thick that cars and trucks had rear-ended ear other, one after another, at high rates of speed. There was an intense conflagration.

The raging fire fueled by diesel from a semi-trailer truck loaded with paper burned so hot that the tires from a dump truck melted onto the road.[8] Tarps were being placed over cars in which there were bodies. Families, worried about loved ones who had not made it to work that morning, were showing up at the site desperate for information. Some of the bodies, they learned, weren't even identifiable. It was horrific — and Gordy wanted to help. Gordy and Kathy have helped various organizations in all sorts of ways over the years, and so have their extended families. They and Al have contributed generously to scholarship funds at both Kewaskum High School and St. Norbert. Gordy, in 2011, became active in an organization begun by Charlie Vitchers and Mike Banker, the New York City Fire Department captain, that builds houses for veterans. Both Gordy and Kathy serve on the board of the National Air Disaster Alliance/Foundation, which works for airline and airport safety.

---

[8] Greg Borowski, Dan Benson and Jessica Hanson, "10 die in horrific pileup." Milwaukee Journal Sentinel, Oct. 12, 2002.

He and Kathy were also certified with the Red Cross, a decision prompted by everything the Red Cross did to help and support the families in New York after Sept. 11. This, though, on the foggy morning of the crash, was a Salvation Army response. Gordy didn't work for the Salvation Army — not really.

That wasn't going to impede him.

"I want to go help," JoEllen heard Gordy say on the other end of the phone. "I want to go help."

Help with what? JoEllen wondered. It was her day off and she had to call her boss to see what — if anything — the Salvation Army was doing to respond. She told Gordy to wait until they heard more about how they could assist. But Gordy didn't want to wait. He called back again, just a little bit later.

"What's going on? Why aren't we going?" he wanted to know.

Gordy can be relentless.

Why does Gordy want to do this? JoEllen was thinking to herself.

Around the third time Gordy called, JoEllen — still without answers for him — decided to give in. She told him to meet her in northern Ozaukee County. From there they would drive to a Salvation Army building a little farther north in Sheboygan County. No sooner were they in the door, than they ran into a Salvation Army officer. Trying to explain why Gordy was there, something she wasn't even sure of, JoEllen mentioned the fact he'd lost his daughter, Andrea, in the World Trade Center attacks the year before.

"Boy, do I have the job for you," the officer responded.

By then it was 8 or 9 p.m. Gordy and JoEllen were led to a room where several others sat around a table: a minister, a police officer and a third man. The man, they quickly came to realize, was just being told that authorities had identified his son's burned body. The man started sobbing, was inconsolable. Nobody around the table knew what to say other than the platitudes that are so often muttered in the face of overwhelming grief. The man's head was hanging down. He couldn't even look up — until Gordy spoke.

Gordy thought when he volunteered that day that he'd maybe end up handing out water bottles to firefighters, or cooking burgers; something like that. Now, he was thinking to himself, *"How do we get through this?"* He started searching his memory bank, asking himself, *"How can I help him?"* Neither Gordy nor JoEllen could remember later everything that Gordy said to the distraught father that day. JoEllen, though, remembered the gist.

"I lost my daughter," Gordy said. "I know exactly how you feel."

The man, paralyzed with grief, lifted his head up and there was an instant bond between the two fathers who had lost their children. Gordy felt more than just a bond, more than just understanding or empathy, though. He had a realization.

"My God," he thought. "I am this guy."

Chapter Twenty-three

Even Gordy has a bit of a hard time explaining his connection to the New York medical examiner's office and the people there charged with telling families their loved ones had been recovered.

"I actually liked — not the right word," he said. "I actually was very comfortable at the M.E's office because most people couldn't get past a certain point. You had to be a family member. I mean there were no tourists around. It is a very quiet and somber place."

Early on, Gordy arranged to have the office contact Mike Meehan, his friend with the New York Police Department, when they would discover something — and then Mike would contact him. In other words, Gordy put a lid on anyone in the medical examiner's office with news about Andrea trying to contact anyone else in the family.

"So," he said, "I would get the calls."

Or he would call them.

The primary medical examiner assigned to Andrea was Katie Sullivan, a woman for whom Gordy has tremendous gratitude. Initially, he'd call Katie every two to three weeks, and eventually about once a month, to talk with her and get an update, see if anything else had been identified. If Katie had something to tell him, the next time he and Kathy were in New York Gordy would excuse himself or leave when Kathy was sleeping and take a cab over. The medical examiner's office had numerous trailers set up, and in each trailer they had trays that were cataloged on a computer. Every "find" was marked on the computer, so Gordy could look and deduce exactly where on the 16-acre site the remains had been found. Everything that was found also had a number. In Andrea's case, there would end up being nine such numbers.

Gordy is aware of the psychological trauma he has gone through, though he doesn't put it that way exactly. The death of a child, of course, is one of the worst things anyone can experience. The murder of a child is another dimension beyond that, though. Then "there are even degrees among people that the less intact the body was, the more trauma their loved ones experienced. They're rewriting the psychology of grief on this," said Gordy.

It's impossible to describe any family of any victim of the Sept. 11 attacks as being fortunate in any way. However, the grief of many of those whose loved ones were never recovered is more pronounced. They would have liked to have had an intact body that could be buried somewhere, or even pieces, some proof, according to Gordy.

Damian Meehan's body was recovered mostly intact on Oct. 1, 2001, from a stairwell that also contained the bodies of firefighters. In a book called "Remembering Inwood's Heroes," his parents called the fact "tragic, yet joyful news" and "a miracle in itself." They were able to have a wake, where thousands showed up, and a funeral and burial. Most other families had much less finality. While some found it easier and better not to have the horrible knowledge that came with knowing where parts of bodies were found, many badly wanted to have any remains at all. Still others, if they had just one number and one bit of evidence, had all they needed. Not Gordy. Gordy wanted, or needed, to find out all of it.

"Why is it important to me? I don't know. I had to. I had to do it," he said.

Why he subjected himself to the knowledge is multifaceted, but starts with, of course, Andrea, and his basic premise that what she endured, he could at least know.

"Anything I had to endure was nothing in comparison to what she was forced to endure," he said.

That is the same reason he traveled thousands of miles for years, went to trials and hearings and anywhere else he could discover the truth, however difficult. He also, though, did it for the rest of his family. The truth of exactly what happened, after all, is inexpressibly painful, and he did not want them to have to know it if they chose not to. He admits he intentionally set himself up as a buffer for others, and still does. But for all that — the fact that Gordy subjected himself to the worst horror a father can imagine and did it for years, does it still — Gordy's investigations and willingness to face the facts are also about himself.

"You have to understand, I did some of this for myself without explaining it to my family," he said.

He seems uncertain about why exactly, although it's possible for an observer to speculate, or just hope, that knowing everything there is to know and reaching the end of that knowledge might help him categorize it and, while never forgetting it, move more fully on to other things in life that have nothing to do with 9/11. In the meantime, though, there is at the heart of much of what he learned a simple truth: What he does know is, to use one of his words, "uncontemplatable."

Andrea's remains, all bone fragments, were recovered between March and May of 2002, although it took a minimum of eight weeks and often as long as a year to identify them. All were recovered at ground zero with the exception of one found in the Fresh Kills Landfill on Staten Island, which served as a sorting ground for much of what was gathered up at the World Trade Center site. He knows much more of the detail, collected all the reports — but prefers to tell a story.

One of his first memories of Andrea, he said one afternoon in the summer of 2011, was of what she looked like before she was even born. Kathy's sister Barb was an x-ray technician at St. Joseph's Hospital in Milwaukee and she took an x-ray of Kathy's belly when Kathy was about seven months pregnant in late 1975. That Christmas, says Gordy, Kathy gave him the "greatest

Christmas gift a father could ever have," a picture of Andrea in the womb.

"Perfect. It was perfect. Head in position. The skeleton. Everything was there, all the parts were there. I was happy."

*   *   *

Part of the dilemma of the 9/11 families was that deconstructing the vast ground zero site, and the Staten Island landfill named after the Fresh Kills Estuary, was a long process that took time. The site workers and the medical examiner's office would keep finding and identifying things, which could create a whole new emergence of grief, and also a basic practical problem. No matter how much was discovered, no matter what the families had to endure, there was for years the looming, never-ending question, "What more?"

"I've talked to a woman. They recovered, and she buried her husband's torso," said Gordy. "Buried his torso and then they found his leg. So what do you do? I mean, impossible questions, uncontemplatable questions. All of a sudden, this is your life at this point."

That's why, in the spring of 2005, Gordy was relieved to get a different sort of call than he normally did from Katie Sullivan. She told Gordy that the identification of victims' remains was being put on hold. Three and a half years after the attacks, everything that could be done already had been done. Portions, at least, of 1,588 victims had been identified by that time, The New York Times reported. [9] Another 1,161 people had never been found. Almost 10,000 unidentified parts had been freeze-dried, vacuum-sealed and preserved in the hope forensic scientists would

---

[9] New York Times, "As 9/11 remains go unnamed, families grieve anew," http://query.nytimes.com/gst/fullpage.html?res=990CEED6163DF937A15751C 0A9639C8B63, (Feb. 24, 2005)

someday have more success. At that point, though, all known DNA technology had been used and exhausted.

Gordy wrote and sent a letter, at that time, to some members of the media in New York and Milwaukee, praising the medical examiner's office and relating some of his feelings:

I received my call concerning the "pause" from Katie Sullivan of the (medical examiner's) office ... about two weeks ago. Katie ... and others at the office have become very special people in my life these last few years.

My daughter Andrea had been in New York for nine hours and inside the North Tower for about forty-five minutes prior to the plane hitting the building. She was in New York on the first business trip of her career, having traveled from her home in Chicago. She knew no one in the New York offices of her employer, Carr Futures. On the 92nd floor, she was trapped with the other 69 people on that floor. Desperate to live, none from that floor survived. The last call out of the tower came from that floor. They were tortured, then murdered. Andrea's and the others' deaths hopefully occurred before being mutilated and scattered amidst that horrible carnage. We drove from our home in Wisconsin with Andrea's fiancé to find her. At that time, we had no proof she was even in the building. And we searched.

None of this makes sense ... still.

Reluctantly we had a memorial service in Wisconsin in late September 2001.

But we had no proof.

That is until May of 2002 when we were notified through the (medical examiner's) office that a piece of her had been identified. We had given DNA samples at the Armory and then additional swabs when we visited the office in April of that year. She was first "found" on St. Patrick's Day in 2002.

As has become my habit, I have called the (medical examiner's) office about every four weeks for updates. And on our numerous trips to New York, we have visited Memorial Park, on the (medical examiner's) grounds to be close to Andy. It is hard to express, as a parent, the horror of this atrocity ... the hesitancy in having a funeral too soon because they may discover more ... the quandary created in our hearts as to the location, so far from home, of her remains. And they have not identified much. But with the call last week from Katie, I am now comfortable knowing that all that could be accomplished has been done.

Throughout these years, my family and I, but most importantly Andrea, have been treated with nothing but the utmost respect, sensitivity and kindness by (members of the medical examiner's) office. I consider them friends.

As an example of their dedication, I remember so clearly the anniversary in 2003. I was honored by New York to serve on the honor guard in the pit that morning. During a break from our duties, I was with some of the (medical examiners). On the bottom of the pit, the earth that remained had been disturbed in preparation for the anniversary. A young man knelt close to the ground and grabbed some of the dirt and started sifting it through his fingers. Others were turning over the earth with their feet and looking down. It hit me like a shot that they were searching for more remains. And I joined them as if it were the most natural, most important task I could be doing. It was crystal clear to me the obligation these people felt: to find and identify the victims in order to bring some peace to the victims' families.

I have come to accept and I am painfully aware that no one involved, in any manner, with the aftermath of 9/11 and the recovery operation will ever be the same. This is especially the case with these good people. I have come to rely on them as a source of strength. I extend to them my sincere and heartfelt thanks and prayers, as I do to so many in New York who we now consider our friends.

I also realize and understand that part of Andrea will remain in New York, perhaps forever. I am comforted that the future care of the rest of her will be under the direction of these fine, sensitive people.

It is now time to bring Andrea home.

-Gordon Haberman, Father of Andrea Lyn Haberman

When the medical examiner's office finally paused the identification process of the remains of the victims, Gordy was asked to give a tribute speech. There were a lot of tears that day. He recognized the dignity the office always accorded the victims and their families, but noted, too, the profound burdens the staff of the office endured themselves for years.

"It was tough on them," said Gordy. "Very few of my contacts can work anymore in the New York ME's office. They've never dealt with anything like this."

No one had.

Chapter Twenty-four

Over time, Kathy came to feel that Andrea — the part of her that had nothing to do with the medical examiner's office — was present in the house in the Town of Farmington where she grew up.

"Andy died but I've learned that she really is with us each and every day," said Kathy, sitting in the kitchen one morning years after the attacks.

Andrea wore a perfume called Happy, by Clinique, and one night Kathy woke up and swore she smelled it. Another time, she says, she was cleaning upstairs and turned to catch a "glimpse" of Andrea's "hair and her T-shirt and blue jeans" as she walked out of the room.

"Now, did that really happen?" asked Kathy, sitting downstairs in the kitchen years later. "I want to say 'Yes,' but maybe I needed it at that time."

Julie, too, has had similar experiences in the house where she and Andrea grew up. Julie and Andrea had their own bedrooms when they were little, and one night in 2005, Julie stayed at her parents' house and slept in her old room. Julie says she is a very light sleeper. She wakes up so easily that she often wears earplugs to bed. But she was not wearing them, she says, when she woke up in the middle of the night and found Andrea sitting on the end of her bed. She felt quite sure she was not dreaming when she saw her older sister there. Andrea had a glow about her and, somehow, appeared "lighter." It was her, though. Julie talked to her the way one sister often does to another, bluntly and with a tinge of sarcasm.

"What are you doing?" she said to Andrea. She said it in a tone, she recalled later, that implied: "It's two o'clock in the morning. Why are you in my room?"

"I'm sitting on your bed," Andrea responded.

"I know," said Julie, "but what are you *doing*?"

I'm visiting you."

"Oh," replied Julie. "Do you do that often?"

"I visit you every night."

Julie, sitting in her own home a few years later, said she often felt Andrea's presence there as well.

"I've always had this sense of — even before this happened with Andrea — just the sense of being very guided or protected, just the very sense that your angels are with you. I don't know. I guess I just always feel like she is with me."

Julie's dreams include a recurrent one in which Andrea talks to her briefly, telling her she doesn't want to stay because she is with God and is OK. There are things, too, that have happened to many people who knew Andrea, or came to know her family after she was killed in New York, that they say seem to be far more than coincidence and are certainly much more tangible than a dream. Andrea, members of her family and others believe, has a connection to them through dimes that they find during what are often very telling times.

Andrea's aunt Shelley — a self-described "skeptic" who started to be open to the possibility of more than coincidence the day she opened the Reader's Digest on the way to New York and saw Andrea's face looking back at her — was the first one to notice dimes turning up after Andrea died. She didn't dwell on it at first, but kept finding them in the middle of rooms, on the floor or outside somewhere, and mentioned it one day to Kathy. It was not long after Sept. 11, and they were wondering where Andrea was, saying to each other, "Where do you think she is?"

You have to understand the way the mind worked after that day, said Shelley. It's not that everyone was in denial about Andrea being dead.

"When somebody vanishes, it's not that you don't know it," she said. "But it does not seem real."

This was not long after the Reader's Digest incident and Shelley was telling Kathy that she thought they should start being open to things they might not have considered before, connections and seeing meaning in things they previously hadn't. She'd barely finished the sentence about finding the dimes when Kathy interrupted and said, "I've been finding dimes, too."

Kathy says she suspects people will think her crazy, but she takes the dimes as a message and reassurance from Andrea, a sign that everything is OK.

One of the most memorable dimes that Kathy found, she says, was in New York. She and Gordy go there every year for Sept. 11. And almost every year, because Andrea liked to shop for shoes, Kathy visits a DSW shoe store.

"Every year I'd walk over there, and I hadn't found any dime at all in New York (that) year, and I was really stressed," she said of Sept. 11, 2008. "So I went over there and I thought I'm going to find one at DSW. I went through the whole thing looking at shoes ... and I was walking in between two aisles of men's shoes. I really wanted an olive-green pair of shoes. I stopped, and here was a pair of olive green shoes in my size in a box. I took one out and tried it on and I thought, 'Ooh, it feels a little bit big.'

"So, I took the other shoe out to put on my foot and there was a dime in the bottom of the box."

Kathy laughed at the memory.

"So," of course, she said, "I did buy the shoes."

A friend has told Kathy that finding dimes is like finding proof that you are surrounded by 10 angels. Gordy describes them as just one of the "God links" they experienced over the years. Shelley describes them simply as "affirmations," messages from Andrea to keep going, to live life, to forge ahead. Shelley and Kathy and Julie — and an ever-growing range of others — have come to believe that the dimes are Andrea's way of trying to let them know she is there.

"I don't want this to be like I am one of these super-converted, spiritual people, because I'm not," said Shelley.

There are some things, though, that have happened that are simple facts, and they involve dimes.

"Maybe there is a way to balance the despair," Shelley started to think early on. "I am not a Pollyanna. There is nothing good about (what happened on Sept. 11). There is nothing positive about this. There is nothing happy about this. But just to be able to manage in your day-to-day life when you see no purpose anymore, I said to Kathy, 'We have to be open to this.'"

Chapter Twenty-five

While they came to feel Andrea's spiritual presence, having something physical was immeasurably important as well. The uncertainty Father Haines felt about whether to grieve the loss or keep hope alive had lingered, after all, well beyond the memorial service in late September of 2001. That uncertainty could finally cease once and for all after Andrea's remains had been recovered and identified. With certainty, however, came other questions, including a frequent one for Kathy.

"Are you," people would ask her when it finally became clear that Andrea was gone, "mad at God?"

"No," she would respond. "I'm not mad at God. No. I believe that human beings didn't do this. I believe that Satan got into the lives of the terrorists and these are satanic people walking around. That's what I believe, because I don't know how any human being can rightfully, in their own mind, blow up other people and themselves. That's not right to me. No, God didn't cause this."

Father Haines, in a discussion years later in the same room where he had met with Gordy and Kathy before the memorial service for Andrea, called it "an interesting question," whether evil is personified in certain people in the world.

Frail human beings do hideous things without being entirely given over to evil, he said. Actions can be pure evil without a person necessarily being so. At the same time, he added, the Catholic Church believes there really is a devil that does act. Evil is a real and tangible force and there are certain people, the Church believes, who have allowed it to overwhelm them to the extent they do become a personification of it.

"Hitler is about as close as we could come," said the priest.

And the terrorists who murdered thousands, including Andrea, on Sept. 11, 2001?

"I don't know if I could go that far. I don't know enough," he said.

"I certainly, on a pastoral level, a very human psychological level, can understand why Kathy needs to say that. There's something about living with the ambiguity and the uncertainty of life, how there can be juxtaposed such great love and such horrible hate, that we end up wanting to tie that up in a bow somehow and not live in the midst of the mess. It's almost like, if you're a believer, there's a part of faith — or one way of looking at faith — that's supposed to take away all that. But there's also another element of faith which allows you to live in the uncertainty of it."

The "mess" is a juxtaposition of incredible evil and incredible love and the difficulty of making sense of it. One way of making sense is through faith, which is quite different than knowing all the answers.

When he was younger, said the priest, he used to attempt to answer when people asked how God allows such evil in the world. He used to respond that there is a reason or a purpose, or he would say that some of it is free will. Now, he just says, "I don't know."

"There's going to be an answer," he said, sitting in the room at St. Frances where he once helped Kathy and Gordy digest what had happened in 2001. "We're going to all ask God that someday. (But) I don't think we can understand it. I don't think it's possible for us as human beings to comprehend that answer."

"The only answer is the cross," he said. "As awful as (things can be), He hasn't abandoned us. That's a sign that he was willing to take it on, too. And that he was willing to suffer the same things we have to undergo.

"The cross is our answer, and it's not an intellectual answer."

Gordy values his crosses, sees the significance in them, and not just in the one that JoEllen gave him after returning from ground zero and having it sliced in half at Ladish. It was Gordy who, walking down Church Street alongside ground zero in 2011, pointed out the enormous iron T-beam, one of several found Sept. 13, 2001, within the rubble of the fallen buildings, which formed a perfect cross.

"Almost immediately," a plaque on Church Street beside the cross explained, "it became a symbol of hope, faith and healing for many rescue and recovery workers searching the WTC site for the remains of thousands who perished in the terrorist attacks. The WTC cross will be housed in the National September 11 Memorial Museum as a testament to spiritual renewal in the face of tragedy and loss."

Gordy, at the same time, is not an adherent of organized religion. Kathy is Catholic, and directly ingrained in the history of the church and its teachings. Gordy says he is "Lutheran, I guess," but he's not really a committed one. At one point, he said, walking down Church Street, he considered joining a different protestant faith closer to Catholicism. At the time, Kathy's mother, the niece of a Catholic cardinal, was ill and in the hospital. Gordy mentioned his and Kathy's trip to the National Cathedral in Washington, D.C., and told Therese that a bishop had prayed with them for her health.

"I am thinking of becoming Episcopalian," he told her.

"It's about time you became something," Therese replied.

Gordy, walking near the cross on Church Street and telling that story, laughed hard at the memory. He has faith, but not the way Kathy does. Julie observes that her father goes about things in a different way than her mother. Even where his faith is concerned, he has to read and know everything he can about both the Bible and the Quran.

Her mom, she said in 2008, is "able to be OK with not knowing. My dad seems to be not able to do that. And then what does he do with all that information?"

Asked at the time if it would make a difference if the United States, for example, found Osama bin Laden, Julie said she didn't know. She did, know, however, that her father felt compelled to try to understand the whole history of al-Qaida and the seeds of how it originated, going back years. So he researched not just what happened exactly to Andrea in her final hours but also the Bible and Christian belief and Islam and history and global politics, all of it in an attempt to find out why Sept. 11 happened. Julie worries that her dad will never get all the answers that he needs. Even when he does get answers, it can be very painful. She also recognizes that, for him, not having the answers is worse than having them because that's just how he is.

Gordy, without diminishing the power of God and His importance to Kathy, concedes he approaches things differently.

Kathy, he said, "has faith. Faith. Not that she wasn't angry, distraught. But her faith never wavered, where I am more analytical."

For some time after the attacks, the yearning for answers focused largely on what happened to Andrea the day she died. That quest never ended. As time went on, though, he also became at least as focused on the people who did it.

"His one last right and act of being a parent for her," said Julie, "is to prosecute and make sure these people are punished and there are answers, and justice is brought to his daughter."

Chapter Twenty-six

Gordy has an office at home that he calls his "war room."

The room is, as he says, "a study in contrasts." Alongside some of his favorite pictures of Andrea, Julie and Kathy, there are numerous shelves of materials devoted to the Sept. 11 attacks: 9/11 Commission reports; legal pleadings and transcripts of various trials; a roll-down map of the Middle East, Northern Africa, Afghanistan and Pakistan; a pin-up board of items he plans to pursue or check on; plus a few hundred books. There are history books, foreign books,   out-of-print books, political books. He has two or three copies of some of them so he can highlight different passages or tear out pages to match other descriptions of the same events in other books in the room. He also has a copy of the Quran, which he is careful not to mark up or desecrate. He also has most of the writings and speeches and warnings of Osama bin Laden.

Gordy needs a bigger office.

"It's cluttered and crowded and getting musty and stinks of too many cigarettes smoked late at night," wrote Gordy in an essay on what he has discovered over the years in that room. "Kathy keeps the door of it closed."

Gordy's journey behind that door — and in courtrooms and the halls of Congress, in Cuba and myriad other places — began as an effort to understand the stunning violence that caused his daughter's death and prompted America to go to war. What type of mentality, he simply wanted to know, could cause this unthinkable act?

Actually, the attacks on 9/11 could have been much worse, wrote Gordy in his essay in the summer of 2011. *If it was bin Laden's intent to kill as many as he could, there were certainly more worthy targets. On the flight path into New York is a nuclear power plant that sits about 35 miles north of Manhattan. Not as big a target as the Trade Center, but it could have potentially rendered Manhattan uninhabitable for a many years if it would have been hit.*

Still, I am stunned at how successful he was.

The toll in the lives of U.S. servicemen and women lost (more than 6,000 and climbing) and injured (almost 45,000 and climbing) since 9/11, the lives disrupted (incalculable) and the trillion dollars we have spent defending Islam from Islam while also trying to protect ourselves from Islam, puts bin Laden right up there as one of the most successful bad guys in history.

This is exactly the situation bin Laden wanted, what he predicted and what he prayed to Allah for. And it was accomplished without an air force, without a tank or a navy or an army in uniform. From what I have read, the entire mission cost about $400,000 dollars and came in under budget. Mohammad Atta and his fellow hijackers were actually refunding extra cash back to al-Qaida operatives in the Mideast until shortly before the attacks.

Amazing.

In the weeks that followed the attack, jihad became a household word that few people understood. Fatwa? What's that? The media bombarded us with every available person who had any type of connection or scrap of knowledge concerning al-Qaida, trying to play catch up on an organization that most never heard of the week before. But most of us still wondered why. Why did they do it?

As the dust still settled on the site of my daughter's murder, I, like most Americans, attempted to fathom the motivations of what to most of us seems like a twisted demonic act of pure evil; an act of evil committed in the name of Allah (The One And Only True God) and of their religious leader, the prophet Mohammed (peace be upon him) and sanctioned by their law, the Quran. I have thought long on how to best approach this subject of what I have learned since Sept. 11, 2001, regarding al-Qaida and the numerous splinter organizations.

What is still difficult to understand is that on any day ... today perhaps; someone somewhere will get up in the morning, and after morning prayers strap on a suicide vest, calmly walk into a crowded bazaar or mall, a post office, a market or fair, an inn or hotel, a place of worship, and shout "Allah Akbar" several times as he or she detonates himself or herself into the next life with 50 or 60 people they likely did not know, nor care about.

That is what I did not understand and needed to find out.

I started out my eulogy at Andy's memorial service by stating "today is not a day to hate..." I still don't hate. There are approximately 1.6 billion Muslims in the world. How does one hate 1.6 billion people? It is very fortunate that those Muslims who do hate us are relatively few in number and are not representative of the nation of Islam.

Bin Laden was damned good at convincing that small group of very motivated, very dangerous, religious fanatics that America was attacking the nation of Islam; convincing them that the actions of the American government are one of the main reasons that the majority of Muslims in the Mideast live in a seemingly perpetual state of strife; convincing them that

America is the reason they live in poverty, with no voice in their governments and without any hope for a future.

The World Trade Center Towers, the Pentagon and what I believe was to be the final target, Congress, were merely symbols of what bin Laden felt contributed to the oppression of the nation of Islam. The Trade Center was attacked for its financial implications of American greed, the Pentagon because of America's power, and Congress was targeted because it is the seat of our country's strength.

Bin Laden did not care who was killed that day. Every religious group in the world was represented in those targets: Muslims, Christians, Hindus, Buddhists.   Similarly, most of those killed and injured in the simultaneous Kenyan and Tanzanian U.S. embassy bombings (at least 323 killed and more than 4,100 injured), which occurred on August 7, 1998, were Muslims by religious affiliation. Some worked in the U.S. embassy; therefore they were fair game and were considered a "takfir," (a Muslim non-believer). Under the belief system of al-Qaida, you can be killed for this. If you happen to be a true Muslim believer, and you happened to be killed walking in the street near the bombing, your reward in heaven is greater. Allah will understand and compensate you in the afterlife.

Wow!

Al-Qaida probably never had more than 500 active members in 2001. While it is now a dead organization, in my estimation, others will fill the void. Al-Qaida and the Taliban trained thousands before the training camps in Afghanistan were shut down. One of the scariest books in my war room is somewhat outdated now. It is titled "A to Z of Jehadi Organizations of Pakistan." Published in 2002, it lists 125 or so different groups. There are probably many more than that now. Many of these organizations are connected or affiliated with madrassas, or schools, that instruct in the Quran and teach and preach the importance of jihad. I have read that jihad is perhaps the sixth pillar of the Islamic faith and that it literally means to strive or struggle. Jihad is an obligation of faith. Simple, right? Christians have pillars of faith, as I would think all religions do. There are different levels of striving and struggle however. The one most Americans should be concerned with is the interpretation of jihad within Islam that deals with the obligation of all Muslims, the faithful of Islam (the ummah) to defend Islam when it is threatened.

America, among many other countries both within Islam and out, threatened Islam in bin Laden's world. He believed and was able to convince many others that violent jihad must be waged not only as a defensive war mechanism but that the struggle needs to be waged until all men submit to Islam. I feel this interpretation is what the extremists within Islam use as justification for their hate and the reason they will continue to plan and plot to not only kill Americans and disrupt our way of life but also apply it to any other Muslims who don't subscribe to this thinking.

Islamic fundamentalists are on a mission from Allah (The One And Only True God), the Prophet Mohammad (peace be upon him) his messenger, and the Quran is their law. Their mission is to defend Islam. That's it.

America is not going to educate the fundamentalists into what we consider to be the errors of their thinking. That is up to the religious leaders of Islam (the ulema) and to the governments of those countries who allow Wahhabi Sunni clerics to spread their "Death to America" message across the Mideast. If anyone thinks Afghanistan and Pakistan are under Western control, they are delusional. America is the Great Satan (next only to Israel) and serves as the scapegoat for brutally repressive governments whose theocratic rulers directly or through their clerical leaders threaten our existence daily, all under the banner of Islam.

It is a credit to our law enforcement community from the FBI down to local police departments that there has not been a successful attack again. Mr. Christmas (the Christmas Day plane bomber, Umar Farouk Abdulmutallab) got very close. Mr. Times Square (Faisal Shahzad) was just not technically savvy enough to detonate his vehicle. It will happen again, not as dramatically as 9/11, but it will happen. Those who mean to harm us will continue to attempt to disrupt our country and our way of life if we give them the opportunity we gave them on Sept. 11.

Chapter Twenty-seven

Gordy needed to see al-Qaida for himself.

In 2006, he and Kathy flew to Alexandria, Va., to attend the trial of Zacarias Moussaoui, the terrorist they came to call "The Moose."

"I never wanted to be a part of history, but was thrust into this. And once thrust into it, I couldn't ignore it. Kathy and I couldn't ignore it," he said.

The Moose was arrested in Minnesota on Aug. 16, 2001. Often inaccurately portrayed as the 20th hijacker, he was reported to the FBI in Minnesota by a flight school operator. It was weeks before Andrea and nearly 3,000 others would be murdered in New York, but no one discovered that because requests from the local FBI in Minnesota to fully investigate him went unheeded by superiors in Washington, D.C.[10] The Moose had not killed anyone, and the FBI didn't know what they had. They did by the time he was tried years later.

Security was heavy both outside and in the courthouse in Virginia in 2006. Courtroom attendees, family members and witnesses were briefed prior to going into court and assigned a "buddy" who sat by their sides. Gordy thought there was probably some concern that someone would jump over a gate and attack The Moose. His own buddy was a gentleman named Harry, who was the chief of intelligence for the National Security Division of the Department of Justice in New York, and Gordy came to admire him greatly.

Gordy had only seen a mug shot of The Moose — until on the first day of the trial when Harry squeezed his leg. He looked up

---

[10] Brian Ross, "FBI Missed Moussaoui Importance," ABC News, Dec. 11, 2001.

and thought to himself, "Well, here is al-Qaida in the flesh." Shackled and heavily guarded, The Moose made a reference to Allah as he looked through the courtroom and at the jurors. He was facing the death penalty. Gordy thought that after years in a stainless steel 10-foot-by-10-foot box and no real contact with anyone from the outside world other than his attorneys, he might be somewhat contrite. Nope. He looked angry, was defiant. In the days ahead, he would sit and glare at others in the courtroom, including Gordy. And Gordy would stare back. They developed what Gordy later quipped was a little "relationship."

Gordy did not attend every day of the trial. He flew back and forth for the parts he wanted to see. He was there, though, on the day prosecutors played the tape from the cockpit voice recorder of Flight 93, the plane that went down in Pennsylvania. This was a great day for The Moose, thought Gordy. Everyone in the courtroom could clearly hear the chaos of the cockpit as the plane was taken over.

"In the name of Allah, the most merciful, the most compassionate," said a terrorist.

Then there was the sound of a scuffle, and voices pleading for life.

"No, no, no, no, no!"

" Please, please, please ... please, please, don't hurt me ... I don't want to die."

After what Gordy came to think of as the sound of death, there was a pause.

"Everything is fine. I finished," said a voice.

While the tape played in the courtroom, Gordy was sitting next to a family member of one of those killed in the cockpit. He noticed that everyone, perhaps without realizing it, was holding on to the benches with white knuckles. Harry had his arm around Gordy's shoulder. Moussaoui just raised his water glass in the air, smiled to the families and to the jury, and said "Allah Akbar."

"This is Islamic fundamentalism," Gordy would later write. "This is the al-Qaida interpretation of jihad. This is their defense of faith.

"This is the threat we face."

Moussaoui pleaded guilty to all the counts against him in 2005, prompting a second, penalty phase of the trial that Gordy also attended. It was during that phase that Gordy learned a lot about Sept. 11. A lot of information had been withheld from release prior to that, a policy Gordy did not view as always necessary. He believed that the secrecy contributed to the mistaken belief among some that the United States government was somehow complicit in the events that occurred that day in 2001.

The Moose was not sentenced to death. He, in the end, was given life in a cell —something he was proud of.

"America, you lost. ...I won," he shouted the day he was sentenced.[11]

The federal judge, Leonie Brinkema, told him those were the last words anyone would hear him say and added that he would "die with a whimper."[12]

Gordy came away from the trial thinking The Moose could not have successfully driven a go-kart into a brick wall. He was not smart enough to run an operation for al-Qaida, but he would have cut your throat in an instant.

Gordy hopes to visit him one day where he is imprisoned in Colorado — along with, perhaps, one other.

*　　*　　*

---

[11] Michael J. Sniffen and Matthew Barakat, *Moussaoui Goes to Prison After Last Taunt*, http://www.washingtonpost.com/wp-dyn/content/article/2006/05/03/AR2006050301661.html (May 2006).
[12] Associated Press, *Moussaoui formally sentenced, still defiant*, http://www.msnbc.msn.com/id/12615601/ns/us_news-security/t/moussaoui-formally-sentenced-still-defiant/ (May 2006).

In December 2008, having already been to Virginia years earlier for Moussaoui's trial, Gordy flew to Seattle to sit in the front row at the sentencing of Ahmed Ressam, the Algerian "Millennium Bomber" who trained at an al-Qaida facility in Afghanistan with Moussaoui. Ressam was captured in Port Angeles, Wash., in December 1999 on his way to detonate a bomb at the Los Angeles International Airport. He, at one point, faced 130 years in prison — a term that was reduced to 22 years as a result of intelligence he initially provided as part of a plea agreement. By the time Gordy went to the sentencing, however, the federal court had reopened the case and prosecutors were arguing for re-imposition of the original penalty because Ressam backed out of the agreement to cooperate with investigators. Gordy, who wanted the original sentence re-imposed, wrote a letter to Ressam and asked that it be entered into the court record by U.S. District Judge John Coughenour.

My name is Gordon Haberman. My beautiful daughter Andrea was murdered along with 3,000 others in New York City. She died a horrific death far away from her family and from those who loved her. I will never forgive.

I have spent the last seven years trying to comprehend why. I have searched for answers and reasons which could explain why you and your kind wish to cause such harm and destruction to innocent people. I am here today because it is important for me to see you despite your not being directly involved with the events of Sept. 11, 2001. It is important to me because you are representative of the organization with intentions that were the same as the animals who perpetrated the atrocity of 9/11. You would wish the world to believe the America wishes your God and his people harm. We do not.

I am extremely grateful that your twisted and flawed plans were thwarted prior to execution. I am grateful that the families of the victims you intended to harm have not had to go through the pain that I and so many others live through every day. Your intention to disrupt our way of life, to injure

and murder as many as you possibly could was intended to
bring America to its knees.

On Sept. 11, 2001, your kind did exactly that.

However, not in the manner you expected, nor in the
manner that those involved on 9/11 intended. We fell to our
knees in prayer. We fell to our knees in hope and faith and
resolution.

Just as you failed, they also failed on Sept. 11, 2001.
Instead, what you and your kind have exposed are the weak,
violent and cowardly followers of equally weak and pathetic
leaders.

You wish us to believe that your religious beliefs provide
you with a reason to destroy those who do not share in those
beliefs. Somehow your beliefs provide you with both a reason
for your wretched existence and a reason to murder even those
of your own faith, those who do not share those beliefs. What
god would command this?

You wish us to believe that our country and the freedoms
that it provides to people of all religions is the reason you and
many of your people live a life of poverty, despair, warfare and
misery. We are not. Your leaders bear responsibility for that
alone. If we are to believe you are a true representative of your
faith and its followers, your religion and your nations will fail.

I have tried to understand your hate. I cannot. What I do
understand, however, is that your message of hate and your
murderous intentions have failed to defeat the ideals and spirit
and faith of this nation. History will only remember your
pathetic life as that of a heinous criminal whose only purpose
was to take that which was not yours, the most precious gift
God has given us all — life.

I have met the finest people of all faiths since 9/11.
However, Islam has suffered greatly because of the twisted
beliefs of those like you. The hopes of its people continue to be
cast to the winds of oppressive and misguided leadership. The
threat they pose to Islam and to the Muslim people is far

greater than the threat your kind poses to us. Americans, along with the vast majority of the people in the world, recoil from the perverse intolerance of radical Islam. We do not hate you. We pity you. We pity the oppression and misery you impose on your people. But beware: We pity you with a vengeance and a strengthened resolve to free those forced to live under this zealous oppression.

As I have indicated, I have attempted to understand you, and what perplexes me the most in your indiscriminate murderous intentions is that you were never harmed by those you intended to hurt. Not in deed, not in thought. You have been protected and attended to while in custody. My understanding is that you promised to cooperate with officials while in custody and then withdrew that promise. I cannot help but wonder if your assistance could have perhaps prevented the atrocity of Sept. 11, 2001 — thereby sparing the life of my daughter and so many thousands of others.

I do know this, however: No matter what sentence this court imposes on you it will be much more compassionate and merciful than the sentence you wished to impose on your intended victims. I will no longer waste any memory of my beautiful daughter on you again. You are not worthy to occupy these thoughts.

Be afraid of your eternity, however. It is hell that awaits you and those who think like you.

　　　　　-Gordon G. Haberman, father of Andrea Lyn Haberman

Much to Gordy's surprise the judge let the reduced sentence stand and even deducted time served — meaning Ressam would be out in 12 years. Gordy was stunned — but pleased to eventually see the U.S. attorney in Washington State appeal the decision. In August of 2011 an appeals court agreed to reconsideration, and Gordy hopes Ressam will ultimately be forced to serve out his original sentence next to The Moose at the federal Supermax penitentiary in Colorado.

Chapter Twenty-eight

By 2005, Gordy knew it wasn't just an occasional, misguided Algerian or Saudi Arabian who expressed or was open to disdain for America. That March, in fact, a student group at the University of Wisconsin-Whitewater, paid almost $5,000 to bring then-University of Colorado-Boulder professor Ward Churchill in to speak and there were protests and rallies both in opposition and in support.

Churchill, an Illinois native, was a terrorist-apologist who, in the days immediately after 9/11, penned an essay labeling the victims of the attacks "little Eichmanns," a reference to the infamous Nazi, Adolf Eichmann, the SS lieutenant-colonel who was head of the Jewish Office of the Gestapo that implemented the mass murder of millions of Jews during World War II.[13]

Initially, there wasn't much attention paid to the ramblings and most media coverage of the essay never did go much beyond that Eichmann reference. The full essay — entitled "Some People Push Back: On the Justice of Roosting Chickens" — proved it was not just a slip of the pen, however. To Churchill, the terrorists were patient and restrained and responding in kind, while the murder victims were somehow responsible for "the starved and rotting flesh of infants." Wrote Churchill in that same essay:

The most that can honestly be said of those involved on September 11 is that they finally responded in kind to some of

---

[13] *Adolf Eichmann,* 1906-1962,
http://www.jewishvirtuallibrary.org/jsource/Holocaust/eichmann.html.

what this country has dispensed to their people as a matter of course. [14]

That they waited so long to do so is, notwithstanding the 1993 action at the WTC, more than anything a testament to their patience and restraint.

They did not license themselves to "target innocent civilians."

There is simply no argument to be made that the Pentagon personnel killed on September 11 fill that bill. The building and those inside comprised military targets, pure and simple. As to those in the World Trade Center ...

Well, really. Let's get a grip here, shall we? True enough, they were civilians of a sort. But innocent? Gimme a break. They formed a technocratic corps at the very heart of America's global financial empire — the "mighty engine of profit" to which the military dimension of U.S. policy has always been enslaved — and they did so both willingly and knowingly. Recourse to "ignorance" — a derivative, after all, of the word "ignore" — counts as less than an excuse among this relatively well-educated elite. To the extent that any of them were unaware of the costs and consequences to others of what they were involved in — and in many cases excelling at — it was because of their absolute refusal to see. More likely, it was because they were too busy braying, incessantly and self-importantly, into their cell phones, arranging power lunches and stock transactions, each of which translated, conveniently out of sight, mind and smelling distance, into the starved and rotting flesh of infants. If there was a better, more effective, or in fact any other way of visiting some penalty befitting their participation upon the little Eichmanns inhabiting the sterile sanctuary of the twin towers, I'd really be interested in hearing about it.

---

[14] Ward Churchill, *Some People Push Back*, http://www.kersplebedeb.com/mystuff/s11/churchill.html. Also at http://la.indymedia.org/news/2005/02/122103.php.

The real marvel was not what Churchill was writing and saying. Crackpots, pseudo-intellectuals and bomb-throwers are a dime a dozen. The real marvel was how many were willing to pay that dime — and a whole lot more — to listen to him. [15]

A UW-Whitewater spokesman stressed that no tax dollars would be spent, but there were others more than willing to pay. The school's Native American Cultural Awareness Association gave Churchill $1,000 to speak. The Black Student Union gave him an additional $400. Donors to the school, most of whom probably didn't know where their money was going specifically, kicked in another $2,600 — and that was just in speaker's fees. There were also bills for Churchill's airline ticket and hotel, the rent for the center where he spoke and miscellaneous other expenses. The total cost of the speech, in the end, was at least $4,880. [16]

Churchill did not back down during his stop in Wisconsin. According to a story in the Capital Times in Madison — perhaps the only paper in America further to the left than Ward Churchill, some would joke — he was "defiant" and "bold" and "passionate." [17] There was a "rapt-capacity crowd," according to the Capitol Times, of about 550 present. The Milwaukee Journal Sentinel reported, in the meantime, that there were about 150 people protesting and about 100 rallying in support. [18]

He said he used the term "little Eichmanns," the Capitol Times reported, symbolically to describe a "technocratic war of empire."

"If Churchill made a mistake with his polemic, he said, it was to assume the general population would be conversant with who

---

[15] Mike Nichols, "Speech's cost far higher than its value" *Milwaukee Journal Sentinel,* 1 March 2005.

[16] Nichols, "Speech's cost far higher than its value."

[17] "Churchill Defends 9/11-Nazi Link," *The Capital Times,* 2 March 2005.

[18] Tom Held and Nahal Toosi, "Churchill defends Sept. 11 essay in speech at UW-Whitewater. Peaceful protests held during Colorado professor's visit," *Milwaukee Journal Sentinel*, March 2, 2005.

Eichmann was and what he did," according to the Capital Times article by Samara Kalk Derby.[19] Churchill said Eichmann just "sat in a bureau in Berlin and arranged train schedules and logistics to make the Final Solution possible" and called him "a nondescript little bureaucrat who was entirely proficient at his job, who didn't even believe in the policy he was implementing."

The professor denied, according to the Capitol Times article, stating that the Sept. 11 attacks were justified, despite the name of the essay: "Some People Push Back: On the Justice of Roosting Chickens." The paper also noted that he had been invited to speak six months earlier about racism against American Indians, and reported that it was only after he'd been invited that his 9/11 essay starting garnering attention around the county. It was the 9/11 message, however, that many clearly came to hear, and commented upon afterward: According to the Capital Times:

> Afterward, (a UW-Whitewater history major) called it a great lecture. "His main theme is that the U.S. should adhere to international law and it would solve a lot of the problems we have today — like terrorism and resentment for the United States."

> "I think he's awesome," (a junior marketing major) said, adding that she was glad Churchill focused on 9/11 and clarified the brouhaha surrounding what he had written.

> "The media tend to make things untruthful by making things controversial," (she) said, adding that her father, a "huge neocon,"

---

[19] Churchill Defends 9/11-Nazi Link," *The Capital Times,* 2 March 2005.

hates Churchill, but she doubts he's read
anything by him.

"He outsources his thinking," she joked
about her father.

Andrea's father, in the meantime, was unimpressed, and
appeared unruffled. Gordy said publicly that guys like Churchill
are simply going to fall of their own weight. But at 2:52 a.m. in
the morning, just hours after Churchill had finished the speech
and collected his applause in Wisconsin, Gordy sent an e-mail to
some members of the local media confessing to a little bit of
anger.

"It is unfortunate that a person such as Ward Churchill had
been given the venue of a university to spread his spurious and
outrageous comments defending the actions of the hijackers that
morning," Gordy wrote.

He noted that "the ramblings of this discredited professor
are neither new, original nor creative. ... Bin Laden has been
spewing this same diatribe for years."

Then, he added:

"Andrea went to work that morning, as did 3,000 others. His
comparison to the Nazis and Eichmann are meant to be
inflammatory but they defy rational thought. These statements
also point to his ignorance of the reality, and of the aftermath of
shattered lives, families and dreams that the cowardly attack of
September 11, 2001, has wrought."

Gordy and Kathy did not attend the speech at UW-
Whitewater. In order to "make some sense and maintain some
balance of the carnage," they instead spent the evening that
Churchill was in Whitewater meeting with a friend from New
York who was passing through Milwaukee. They discussed an
interim Sept. 11 memorial that was being planned for a location
next to New York Fire Department's famous Ladder 10 and
Engine 10 companies — the 10-10 — across from the Trade

Center site. The 10-10 lost five firefighters that day. The temporary memorial was to act as an educational site for visitors to ground zero and also serve as a spot where survivors and families could meet until the permanent memorial was completed. It was a way of helping remember the many victims for who they really were.

"For us," noted Gordy, "this was a productive way to counter the occasion of Ward Churchill's speech."

As for Churchill, wrote Gordy in his late-night, 2005 e-mail: "I believe Churchill's venues to speak will begin to disappear and he will fall of his own weight into oblivion."

Six years later, after losing his $96,000-a-year job at the University of Colorado and as the legal tussle resulting from that firing continued to work its way through the courts, it appeared the professor had done just that.

Chapter Twenty-nine

Jessica, the woman who had tried to help find Andrea in the days after the attacks, was in some ways the polar opposite of Ward Churchill and those who rallied in support of him at Whitewater. While Churchill's instinct was to deride the victims of 9/11, hers was to search for and try to embrace them — a reaction partly due to the fact she personally witnessed the attacks and what followed.

In the immediate aftermath of the attacks, while Churchill was comparing the victims to a Nazi mass murderer, she and her roommate Brendan, the carriage driver she had met on her first visit to New York and a guy who had become her close friend, were trying to clean up the grayish-brown ash that had covered their grill and furniture and backyard in Red Hook. Brendan, who Jessica thought of as the chattiest guy on earth, was the quietest Jessica had ever seen him. Wearing masks and using shovels the day after the attack, the two of them worked in silence to clean up their portion of the Brooklyn neighborhood that sat along the waterfront and faced downtown Manhattan. It was only years later that they discovered they were, at the time, thinking the exact same thought.

Were we cleaning up the ash of a human being? Were we breathing a human being into our lungs?

Sitting in a tea shop in downtown West Bend, the Wisconsin hometown to which she eventually returned, Jessica said in 2011 that she thought Midwesterners had a visual understanding of what happened on Sept. 11 in New York. It usually stemmed, though, from what they had seen on TVs that could be turned off. In New York, there was never such a switch. Sept.11 infused everything in your life, often literally. The ash wasn't just in their backyard. It had worked its way into their house, their kitchen and their clothes. Months later, Jessica would be walking down the street and suddenly smell the fire and the invisible cloud it had left hanging thick over the city.

You didn't have to be there on Sept. 11, though, or know Andrea while she lived, to come to understand at least some of the impact of the tragedy.

Becky Bilbrey, a young woman who'd been living in Minnesota in 2001, came to understand it through what she thinks of as a profound and more than coincidental encounter with Gordy and Shelley.

Becky didn't move to New York until 2004 and visited ground zero on Sept. 11 that year. She was in media sales at the time and had to work that day, so she didn't arrive at the site until the sun was going down on what was a beautiful, early evening. One of the cruel juxtapositions of Sept. 11, 2001, has always been that it was as close to perfect an autumn day as anyone could remember and Sept. 11, 2004, was equally as memorable. So many people were gone, so many thousands of lives lost, that it could be difficult to get one's mind around the enormity of what had happened, especially on a pristine and lovely day three years later. Becky walked around lower Manhattan that evening, trying to digest it all. She stopped and read many of the letters and tributes to the victims that were taped to fences and buildings all around ground zero, trying to understand what and who had been lost, what it meant, how it changed things. She was alone that evening and, because it was nightfall and the ceremonies were over, the area had mostly cleared out. Almost everyone had left. She decided to leave as well, to meet her boyfriend. But at the last moment, after the sun had set behind the skyscrapers that remained, she noticed two people, a man and a woman, standing near a fence along the perimeter of the site, not far from the 10-10 quarters on Liberty Street.

The man and the woman were together, but otherwise all alone. The street, but for them, was completely empty. Becky, immediately struck, stood back and watched them. The man was standing there, silently watching while the woman used purple and white ribbons to tie a bouquet of yellow roses to the fence underneath a photo. She was taking her time, intricately tying the ribbons with great precision and care, making sure everything was perfect. To Becky, their pain was palpable.

Becky simply stood there at first, not wanting to intrude, mesmerized and barely able to breathe. She was touched and curious, and after they were done gently affixing the ribbon and picture to the fence and had started walking away, she went over and looked at the photo. It was tiny, only about 3 inches by 2 inches, something you wouldn't normally notice in the vastness of the city. It was a picture of a very young, very pretty young woman with long, brown hair and a joyful smile who probably would have been about Becky's age had she lived.

Then she looked closer and realized the girl in the picture wasn't just *about* her age.

"We love you Andrea," it said by the picture. "We will never forget." Below those words, she noticed, there was also a birth date and a date of death:

"2/2/76 – 9/11/01."

Becky was immediately engulfed by emotion. She herself had been born on Feb. 2, 1976. This girl, Andrea, had been born on the same day and in the same year she had been: 2/2/76. Becky had never in her entire life met anyone with whom she shared her exact birthday. Struck by the coincidence, feeling herself actually tremble, she turned and called out to the woman who had been taking such time with the bows and flowers and who was now walking away.

"I'm sorry, ma'am, excuse me," she called out. "Excuse me … Is this your daughter?'"

"No, it's my niece," said the woman, who was slender, had brown-hair and was in her forties.

"I'm so sorry to bother you, but I just have to tell you. We have the exact same birthday. I was born on the same day. I have never known anyone with my birthday."

"Oh, my goodness! Oh my goodness!" said the woman, asking Becky what her name was. "Will you please come speak to her father? Please come speak to her father."

Gordy had walked ahead a little, and Shelley rushed to get him and bring him back to where Becky stood. She explained what had happened. Becky told them how sorry she was about Andrea, this girl she'd never met, and then, without being able to say much more, started sobbing. Instead of her consoling them, they started to console her; hugged her and told her it was OK. All she could get out, in the meantime, was how sorry she was and that she would pray for them. What she felt and couldn't express until much later, though, was something much more. She believed that they were present for her that day just so that she could understand what and who had been lost, what really happened on Sept. 11.

"You hear about it and you read the stories and you watch the news, but you don't understand until you've actually met someone who's been through it," she said later. "It just seems like a story someone told you. You can't compute that kind of tragic horror. You can't even conceptualize it until you've actually been around someone and felt their pain and suffering. I don't know if that was just something I needed to learn as a human being, something I needed to understand as a person."

The mathematicians say that the chance any one person you encounter will share your exact birthday is about 28,000 to 1. Becky felt that the chances of coming across a picture of a girl with her exact birthday and also meeting her family on a late evening when nobody else was present in a spot that can normally be extremely crowded were probably more like a trillion to one.

The emotional conversation didn't last long, but before they parted, the man and the woman left her with a few words. It was, of course, only September, still five months away from Feb. 2, Becky's and Andrea's birthday. But the man, Gordy, spoke to her in a soft voice that seemed to carry a special resonance. It was Shelley who later remembered Gordy's words:

"Have a nice birthday," he said.

Becky is now an actress living in California. On that day, though, because she was still in the business world, she was dressed in a dark suit. She was wearing pumps and carrying a briefcase, like Andrea might have. She did not seem like a child or someone unable to take care of herself —quite the opposite — but Shelley felt compelled to tell her something before she "melted into the night."

"Please be careful," Shelley said to Becky. "Please get home safe."

Both women felt the poignancy of that moment.

"There was something about Becky and this encounter at the end of a long, emotional day. You just don't see this stuff coming," said Shelley.

After some time and another coincidental meeting with a different friend of the Habermans, Becky became close to Shelley. And through Shelley, Becky remained in touch with Gordy as well. When Becky and her husband, Ryan, moved to Los Angeles, they stopped to visit Shelley in Wisconsin. Becky has a picture of Andrea in her wallet and keeps one on her dresser as well. She would later come to rely on Gordy for advice and support during a difficult time in her life.

In January 2009, Becky and Ryan were in Park City, Utah, for the opening weekend of the Sundance Film Festival, and were attacked. Ryan ended up at the University of Utah Hospital and required three surgeries to repair fractures to his cheekbones and have plates put into his eye sockets. To this day, he has 26 screws and eight titanium plates holding his face together, according to Becky. The Park City newspaper, the Park Record, called it a "shocking episode of violence on Main Street," a disheartening one, too, because the main attacker ended up serving only 230 days in jail. Gordy, Becky said, was a "huge help" and support through it all.

"I was very discouraged because we didn't get the outcome that we wanted," said Becky. "I was just so down about it, and I remember Gordon sending me an e-mail and telling me that justice doesn't always happen when we want it to."

Mostly, though, he helped them realize something else.

Gordy, she said, demonstrates "the ability to wake up every day and the ability to fight and to work and to ... just keep the hope alive." So many people in their situation "would just absolutely crumble and not be able to move forward. I don't know how I would," she said. "I don't even know how they deal with it, but they've dealt with it with a grace that is unexplainable and have been an inspiration to so many people," including those who weren't anywhere near New York on Sept. 11, 2001, and whose suffering is of a wholly different origin.

Chapter Thirty

Gordy, as he suggested to Becky, knew well about the fickleness of justice, and so did Al. To Al, the terrorist attacks were, quite simply, an act of cowardice.

"You know," he said one evening in 2008, what they did was carried out "against helpless people, and that really bothers me." Andrea "didn't have anything to do with it. She wasn't prepared. You know, the hatefulness really bothers me. Then the violence of it: I know innocent people die every day, but usually it's by accident. You know there's violence in the world, but not on such a mass scale like that. That kind of pisses me off.

"So you know it bothers me every time I get on a plane. I want there to be a hijacker on it.

"I think I would be more than happy to sacrifice myself to not let it happen again. You know, if I had to take a bullet or knife or something like that, I'd be more than happy, so that nobody else had to go through this same shit. So that's what I always think of. I always pick an aisle seat and keep an eye out for people walking up and down the aisle."

Al was not the only one who wanted justice over the years.

Gordy and Kathy didn't take many pictures in New York during the days immediately after Sept. 11. One shot they did take, though, was of the message spray-painted in red and black on a piece of machinery not far from ground zero: "bin LADEN MUST DIE!" it said.

When they returned home with the realization Andrea had been murdered, they blew that picture up and placed a large copy above their fireplace. It hung in that same spot for more than nine long years, until the morning of Monday, May 2, 2011, right after news broke that bin Laden had been killed hours earlier by U.S. forces in Pakistan. Kathy got up from the kitchen table that morning, walked over to the picture and took it down so they could take a closer look. Gordy sat at the table just feet from where he had watched the towers burning on TV in 2001.

"My first thought" after hearing that bin Laden had indeed been killed, Gordy said, "was for all the servicemen. There have been over 5,000 Americans killed in this war, probably 5,500. I am very humbled about that. My thoughts go out to them and those injured and their families."

"My first," said Kathy, "was a prayer to God, a thank you. I hope God did not frown on me for thanking him."

The morning after bin Laden was killed in 2011, Julie had a different reaction than her parents. She had heard the news from her fiancé, Troy, who became her rock and, she said, her source of unconditional love in dealing with Andrea's death over the years. She was in her car on the way to work when Troy told her about bin Laden. Perhaps because she was also in her car the morning of Sept. 11, it was "almost like an exact replay," she said. By the time she got to work that Monday, the tears were flowing and "it just put me back nine and a half years ago." It was surreal and very difficult for her, she said. "It took me back. It took my breath away."

Learning about new 9/11 information has become a way of life, she would later note, and something she is accustomed to dealing with. "However, this came as a total surprise and there was no way of protecting myself."

Gordy's concern about and appreciation for American troops would take on even more meaning when, three months later, 30 Americans, including many from the same elite Navy SEALS Team 6 unit that killed bin Laden, died in a Chinook helicopter brought down by terrorists in eastern Afghanistan. The bin Laden mission was so successful, it became apparent in retrospect, that it had been easy for many Americans to gloss over the acute danger, as well as all the uncertainty, that surrounded bin Laden's whereabouts.

"I honestly did not know if he was still alive, or if he was maybe in Saudi Arabia," Gordy said, sitting in the kitchen back in May.

There was that morning, certainly, a sense of relief.

"The world is a better place without (bin Laden)," said Gordy. "No question."

His feelings were nuanced, though. He had spent years investigating not just what happened to Andrea, but studying why bin Laden and his minions did what they did. He had traveled all over the country, been to Washington, D.C., countless times to make sure the politicians did not forget. He had read almost everything bin Laden ever wrote, every speech he ever gave. He had spoken directly to ambassadors and attorneys general of the United States, was in the nation's Capitol speaking with his congressman, Jim Sensenbrenner, just a couple weeks earlier. He had become more than just one victim's father. He'd become a prominent advocate and a vocal one for all the victims that day — and for justice. Part of what he felt immediately after bin Laden's death, he said, was odd.

"I feel like I have lost an adversary after a long hunt," he said.

It was a good and just thing, bin Laden's death, both Gordy and Kathy felt. But they had concerns. Gordy was concerned that morning immediately after the news broke that bin Laden would "be martyred and that there will be events in the United States against American citizens." What he focused on mostly, though, was the fact others were yet to be caught or killed, people like al-Qaida's second-in-command, Ayman al-Zawahiri. Gordy expressed hope that one day he would himself be able to testify at the trial of Khalid Sheikh Mohammed, the mastermind of the attacks, and Walid Bin 'Attash, Ramzi Binalshibh, Ali Abdul Aziz Ali, and Mustafa al Hawsawi — all of whom were to be charged with, among other things, murder.

Gordy had already been to Guantanamo Bay Naval Base by then. He had years earlier been selected from a group of 9/11 family members by lottery to attend hearings on the five who, prosecutors say, are the architects and engineers responsible for the Sept. 11 attacks. He came away convinced that Gitmo and the military justice system was the proper venue for their trial and was planning to go back to Cuba to, hopefully, testify. When Kathy took the picture down off the wall that Monday, the nail behind it bent, so it stayed down for a time. As if in acknowledgment of the fact there was more justice to be sought, though, they soon hung the picture back up. Getting bin Laden — good as it was — was not yet the full measure of justice Andrea and the other victims of Sept. 11 deserved.

"What is justice," asked Kathy, "after he murdered so many people?"

Gordy, sitting at the kitchen table near the same spot he found out about the attacks that killed his daughter almost 10 years earlier, answered the question.

"If we systematically continue to bring these architects and engineers of 9/11 to termination," he said, that will be justice.

Chapter Thirty-one

Maggie Gustafson, who started the Milwaukee chapter of Parents of Murdered Children after her son Tony was killed, is married and has another, younger child. Her family is the same size as the Habermans. She has seen and experienced herself the strain invariably left on marriages and families and surviving children after a murder. She says she is proud, despite the inevitability of that strain, of the way her family came through the tragedy.

She knows that the Habermans have more than good reason to be as well.

"We were a family" through everything, "all of us," said Gordy. Still are. For all the people they reached out to and the support they received elsewhere over the years, it was always the support from each other, he said, that formed the bedrock.

"There was never the tearing apart. We all supported each other and held each other up through phases of grieving," said Kathy. "We all went through terrible periods that some people do not even know about. If not for family, we would not have made it through."

Gordy met Kathy when he was just 15, and is deeply intertwined with her family. He sat in her mother's house in West Allis one summer day in 2011, remarking to his mother-in-law that he'd been hanging out there for about 45 years and recalling how as a teenager he was just "smitten." There will never be anyone else like Kathy, he made it clear. And there will never be anyone else like Julie; never was. Julie, when she was little, was different than her older sister, Gordy said. She never had any fear. Andrea was older but she would actually sit back and wait for her little sister to do something new before she'd try it herself. Julie was not the one who needed encouragement or necessarily wanted help. Gordy remembers watching her practice riding her bike as a little girl and "cringing" inside the house because he wanted to "run out there and get her." But, he says, she mastered the thing before he got there.

"We love our kids for their uniqueness, their individuality, their laughter, for just being them," said Kathy. "No two people are the same or will ever act the same. Every child is a gift from God.

"We knew how extremely hard and difficult and unfair it was for her to watch us as parents be pulled apart at the heart, but we always had that deep love for Julie no matter what. We lost a great deal of Julie and she lost a great deal of us, but we always stuck together. Love is limitless."

It also comes in different varieties.

Not much more than a month after bin Laden was killed in early May, and while Gordy waited to find out if he might be able to personally testify at the trials at the naval base in Cuba at some point, he sat at the same kitchen table with a young man, much younger than Julie or Andrea was when she died, who had heard a little bit about justice but who had learned a whole lot more from Gordy about something else: how to move ahead regardless.

Gordy first met Scott in March 2003, right around the same time the medical examiner's office in New York was identifying the last of what had been recovered of Andrea. Julie was well into her twenties by then and Andrea was gone in a way that was undeniable. Gordy felt he might be able to be something different than a father to a child in need of a friend. He thought he might want to try to be a big brother. He walked into the Big Brothers Big Sisters of Washington County office in West Bend and said he wanted to volunteer. He didn't have a grand plan. Had no idea who might need his help. He just thought it might be nice to spend some time with someone young who didn't have all the support he and his family had.

They don't take just anybody off the street at BBBS. They conduct a background check and do an interview and make sure you know you're making a long-term commitment. And when it came to Scott they were even more deliberate and careful. Mary

Gamerdinger, the BBBS director, knew she needed to find somebody whom she could trust implicitly, maybe somebody a little older and settled in life who would definitely stick around. She couldn't have fathomed finding somebody who had not just all those qualities but an understanding of the sort of trauma Scott had himself been through.

Scott was 13 at the time, one of the older "Littles" as BBBS calls the kids. Mary saw him as somewhat quiet and reserved, not somebody to just dive in and open up to people, but also intelligent and inquisitive. He was a kid who was going to ask questions, some of which, she knew, might be unusually tough because of the reason Scott needed a Big Brother in the first place. Eight years earlier, in August 1995, his father was shot and killed while getting out of a car in the parking lot outside his office in Phoenix, Ariz. Although Scott's parents had divorced earlier that year, and his mother was already remarried by the time of the shooting, she was still the beneficiary on Scott's father's $250,000 life insurance policy, according to court records. It took about a year but Scott's mother and her husband were arrested in Jamaica and charged, along with two others, with being part of a four-person conspiracy to commit the murder and collect the life insurance proceeds.

All four were eventually convicted. Her husband, found guilty of conspiracy to commit murder and murder in the first degree, received the longest sentence: life in prison with no possibility for parole or release. Scott's mother ended up with one of the shorter ones. She steadfastly denied having any knowledge of the murder or conspiracy and the jury at her trial came back hung on the charges of conspiracy to commit murder and murder in the first degree. After that, she entered a no contest plea to a reduced charge of manslaughter and was sentenced to 12 years.

Scott had gone to live with his paternal grandparents by then; and after his grandfather died they decided to move back to his grandmother's home state of Wisconsin. It was then that she realized he might benefit from having a male presence in his life. She ended up approaching Big Brothers Big Sisters at almost the same time Gordy did, a bit of fortuitousness that many of those involved came to feel changed Scott's life.

"You know, we work with hundreds of amazing volunteers every year and we meet hundreds of kids, all of whom are wonderful and have a lot of potential that just needs to be brought out," said Mary, of BBBS. But "every now and then you see a child or a volunteer or a match that just stands out as exceptional or touches your heart a little bit stronger."

Scott seemed to immediately take to this man with the beard, the deep voice and a manner that could alternate between jocularity and serious conversation. After an initial "match meeting" at the home of Scott's grandmother, said Mary, a BBBS staffer came back and told her two things: Gordy was still there playing chess with Scott, and the match had given the staffer "goose bumps."

Gordy and Scott became buddies, and more.

Thursday was always the day, when everyone was younger, that Gordy set aside for his daughters. Gordy came to think of Thursdays as "no rule day," a chance to just kick back and do little-kid stuff. They'd go to a movie or go bowling, or just goof around. Sometimes he'd even pull them out of school. "And we'd just have fun," he said. "I had determined that that was going to be a fun day in our life and an important time."

After Gordy became a "Big," he and the new kid in his life got together on Thursdays to hang out. He and Scott went to Brewers games, went fishing. Several times, they took a plane ride from the West Bend Municipal Airport. They drove up north and planted trees. They also talked about all the really important stuff in a teenage boy's life, such as cars.

Cars were important to Scott. He always had a job or two at places such as Culver's or a garden center, and he had a little money, though not enough to buy the car he wanted when he turned 16. He had his eye on a used 2006 Scion tC, and had scraped together most of the money he needed. He liked it because it got good gas mileage, was getting good reviews and was in his ballpark on price — almost.

"I remember," he said, "we were sitting there talking about the price, and what the deal was. ... I remember I put probably around $2,000 from my own savings that I just collected over the years. I needed a little bit more, and my grandma and Gordon were there, and we were just talking about it and I kept asking Gordon and Grandma, 'Do you think I should do it?'"

"Well, if you want to do it," said Gordy after considerable discussion, "you can."

Gordy told Scott he wanted to make up the difference between what the car cost and what Scott had on hand. Gordy, Scott said, kicked in a substantial amount of money out of his own pocket. It was, he said, "pretty overwhelming."

Not everything was easy with Scott. He had his share of trouble. He veered off course enough that his grandmother wondered if Gordy would just give up on him. Gordy didn't.

"I think it really meant something," she said, "that Gordy did not walk away."

"As Scott got older I think the thing they did most often was just go out and talk and it was amazing how long they could talk for an adult and a teenager," said Mary. "They were so interested in each other's activities and in their thoughts and exchanging opinions on things without judgment. I think Scott got to feel very open, that he could say whatever he truly thought or felt or ask for help on whatever he needed, and that, despite the ups and downs of a friendship or a relationship, Gordon was going to be there. He was just a role model on so many different" levels.

Scott, sitting in Gordy's kitchen in 2011, eight years after they first met, realized in retrospect the influence Gordy had on him.

"I would say that he's made a dramatic impact on what my beliefs were then, versus what they are now," he said. "He always had an answer to any question I had. Not too many people did, because I'd ask really complex questions. So, I'd have my own thoughts on particular things. But he just, whenever I had a really perplexing situation, he was able to point out a good way to approach it."

When Scott was younger his grandmother didn't tell him a lot about what had happened. By the time Scott was 16, however, she'd told him everything because when a child gets to a certain age "there is no point in hiding that stuff," she said.

One of those perplexing questions Scott had for Gordy was how do you take a tragedy, "any given tragedy," and "not let it affect everything in your life? How do you manage it without keeping things inside to the point where it may be a hazard to you?" How, in essence, do you "deal with things?"

Part of what helps, Gordy made it plain, is knowing there are others who have experienced deep grief.

"We don't have a lock on grief," says Gordy. We are "not unique."

Sept. 11, 2001, fundamentally changed the way he and Kathy thought about life. Up until then, it had a certain predictability and comfort and definite direction to it. That is not, though, the way life often turns out. It throws you curveballs and life becomes more about living in the present than the future — or the past.

"A lot of times," said Scott, "we arrived at just being preoccupied and just living in the now, instead of the then. And that really helps you move on, when you think like that."

By 2011, Scott had graduated from high school, gone on to earn an associate's degree in software applications and programming, and was working toward a bachelor's degree related to information security systems. He had become, in his grandmother's words, "a goal-setter," "responsible," a "penny-pincher," a young man with a positive attitude headed in the right direction. "I believe a lot of that," she said, "is on Gordy's shoulders."

"We both experienced this hardship," said Scott. "Could have taken it the bad way. Perhaps, when he first met me, I didn't … really understand what would be the reason for good, why people still do good. And he has really helped to show me that, as he told me once, it's not what curveballs you get in life, it's how you hit them."

Chapter Thirty-two

The last time Gordy and Kathy ever saw Andrea was on Labor Day 2001, eight days before she was to be in New York.

Gordy was concerned about her going to the Carr offices in the World Trade Center. But they were all concerned, too, about something else that day. Morgan, the golden retriever Andrea and Julie had grown up with, was old and not healthy. Dogs have always been a focal point for the Habermans and, even more so, for Kathy's family. Her sister Terry has horses and therapy dogs, and shared her love of animals with Andrea. Andrea even had a paw-print tattoo on her right ankle.

"Give Morgan a hug," Gordy said to Andrea as she was walking down the driveway, "because you never know if you are going to see him again."

Andrea did. She got down on her knees in the front yard and hugged Morgan and then said goodbye and got in the car and drove back to Chicago, and went off to New York a week later.

That final exchange came back to Gordy often, including the day he was in New York standing outside St. Vincent's Hospital after the towers had gone down. He suddenly heard sirens moving up from ground zero.

"You could hear them blocks away, and everybody's head snapped in that direction," he said. "Medical units started getting ready."

The immediate hope was that people had been found alive at ground zero and were being transported on the flatbed truck speeding up Broadway. He then realized the sirens were not for survivors. There were two dogs on the truck, a German shepherd and a golden retriever, like Morgan. Both were on their backs with their feet up in the air. It occurred to Gordy later that they'd been burned. At the time, he didn't realize how hot the site was, or how relentless rescue dogs can be. All he knew was that he was bothered by what he saw.

"What I didn't know is that they would go until they hurt themselves" and not just physically, Gordy said later. The rescue dogs "would get incredibly depressed and could even die of depression because they couldn't find anybody."

The other thing he later learned: Rescue dogs are specialists. They search for live people or for cadavers, either the living or the dead, but not both. Searching for both would be too confusing. Most of the dogs used in the early days, including, most likely, the ones Gordy saw on the flatbed truck after suffering burns to their paws and bellies, were live-scent dogs. They searched only for people who were alive, which would explain their injuries. They'd have been on the site, not finding anybody, but wouldn't stop looking until forced to stop.

"They had to pull them off the pile and reinforce their training by letting them find live people," said Gordy. "I can understand that."

In April 2002, before they knew any part of Andrea had been recovered, Gordy, Kathy and Shelley decided that one of the things they wanted to do was help sponsor a rescue dog of their own. They contacted the National Disaster Search Dog Foundation (SDF), which had sent 13 dogs to the WTC, none of which were injured. It is expensive to train a rescue dog and its handler, generally about $15,000, and the organization is constantly in need of money. After having dinner with SDF representatives in New York that spring, all of them made donations, and Kathy's family became frequent givers as well in the years that followed.

Wilma Melville, SFD founder and a longtime FEMA-certified handler, remembers standing in front of the Alfred P. Murrah Federal Building in Oklahoma City with her dog after the bombing in 1995, and wanting to find a way to balance out what she calls "the evil" that had been done there. At the time, there were only 15 certified handlers in the entire country. Shortly after that, she founded SDF, which by the summer of 2011 had trained well over 100 dog-and-handler teams, and more than 70 of those were active.

Her first recollection of the Habermans after the Sept. 11 attacks was that they were "beyond belief heartbroken," and searching for some way "to get out from under this terrible grief."

In addition to making consistent contributions to the organization, the Habermans helped raise funds and made an appeal to other 9/11 families. They also forged a bond with one dog in particular. About that same time the family became interested in SDF, a golden retriever with all the qualities of a search dog was rescued from a shelter in, coincidentally, Wisconsin.

SDF decided to name him Andy

Andy searches for the living, and he is relentless.

"I remember when Andy the dog was young I would get reports that he can eat through walls. He will eat through walls to find somebody that he is searching for," said Gordy. "He will go through concrete. He will find a way."

"Very determined, focused is a good way to describe him. Nothing really will stop him from finding the person that he looking for," said Russell Tao, Andy's handler, a firefighter-paramedic with California's Chino Valley Fire District.

Andy was used in the aftermath of Hurricanes Gustav and Ike along the Gulf Coast in 2008. He never had the opportunity to find a survivor. But Russell flew with him to Wisconsin in the summer of 2010 and took him to Gordy and Kathy's house and demonstrated both what he is capable of and the reason he has always given hope to those preparing for future tragedy. Andy, 10 years old by then, was being retired, and Gordy and Kathy expressed some interest in taking him after that. A rescue dog is a different sort of animal than a pet, though, and Andy just didn't mesh with the Habermans' other two dogs. So Russell decided to keep Andy with him and his family in California, a decision that turned out to have certain symmetry to it.

Russell has a daughter, Emma, who was 2 years old the summer of 2011 and is crazy about Andy. "Loves him to death," according to Russell.

"The way it worked out is our daughter is taking care of Andy now," he said.

Back in Wisconsin, it turned out that Morgan lived a lot longer than anyone expected after that day when Andrea hugged him and walked down the driveway for the last time. Morgan lived about three years beyond 2001 before dying as well.

In California during the summer of 2011, though, a different little girl was hugging another golden retriever who, it so happens, came from Wisconsin.

Chapter Thirty-three

In the summer of 2011, six weeks after Osama bin Laden had been killed and not long before the 10th anniversary of the attacks, Gordy sat on a bench in front of the Amish Market, where Tricia Perrine had stopped at the last moment on Sept. 11 to get a bagel instead of walking into the north tower to meet Andrea — inadvertently saving her own life.

Tricia, by late summer that year, was working for a hedge fund in Connecticut, and she was married and expecting her second child. The market had long since been rebuilt and was flourishing, while just a block away, work continued apace on the 1 World Trade Center building and the National September 11 Memorial and Museum being built within the footprints of the twin towers. Andrea's name, along with the names of nearly 3,000 others who died in the 2001 attacks and in the 1993 bombing she wrote about in high school, were being inscribed on bronze panels that were to line reflecting pools at the memorial. Gordy had, by then, agreed to give Andrea's clutch purse to the museum, where it will become a part of history. The hope of those who planning the memorial and the museum is that the purse and other things recovered from the site will become cause for reflection.

The Habermans who had already spent many years remembering Andrea at that site, found themselves thrust from a small, largely rural town in Wisconsin into the epicenter of one of the most significant and transformative events in U.S. history. Sitting on the bench out in front of the Amish Market, Gordy recalled being asked to read names of victims at the first anniversary ceremony. He stood on a dais at ground zero in front of a crowd of thousands of people. A large contingent of family members had flown out that day to be with Gordy, Kathy, Julie and Al, including Al's family; Kathy's brother Kenny; her mom,

Therese; Gordy's sister, Shelley; and Kathy's sisters, Patty, Terry and Barb. Barb was dying of cancer at the time, but insisted on being there. She stood in the crowd in pain and listened to the names being read for three full hours.

On the dais, the organizers of the ceremony paired family members who were reading names with well-known New Yorkers. Gordy was paired with Ray Kelly, the New York City police commissioner. Ed Koch, former New York mayor, and Hillary Clinton, then a New York senator, were sitting nearby. Mayor Michael Bloomberg and then-Gov. George Petaki were standing in an aisle. A short distance away sat film director Stephen Spielberg and actor Robert De Niro, who was wiping tears from his eyes. Many of the names of the victims being read were foreign-sounding — testament to the ethnic and religious diversity of the dead, indeed of New York itself.

Sitting outside the Amish Market, Gordy recalled being worried that when it came his time came to read, he would mispronounce some of the names, and mentioned that to Kelly. Immediately, translators showed up and wrote down phonetic pronunciations for all of the name-readers.

"What's in a name?" said Gordy, thinking back. "Everything, at that point."

Many of the families whose loved ones weren't recovered "had nothing else," he said.

"I learned very quickly at that point that there are certain people, like Ray Kelly, who can get things done quickly. Fortunately, he understood and recognized what was important, and not just on that day."

Gordy read names often at the site in the years after that, as would Julie, Al and Shelley, as well as Charlie Vitchers. After that first year, they would get CDs with pronunciations on them well ahead of time. That first year, though, the pronunciations were just written by the translators on the sheets themselves. Gordy alternated reading names with the police commissioner.

Gordy stood at one podium and read the first name, "Katsuyuki Hirai."

Ray Kelly stood at another and read the second name, "Heather Malia Ho."

And then they alternated:

"Tara Yvette Hobbs."

"Thomas Anderson Hobbs."

"James J. Hobin."

"Robert Wayne Hobson."

"Dajuan Hodges."

"Ronald George Hoerner."

"Patrick A. Hoey."

"John A. Hofer."

"Marcia Hoffman."

"Stephen G. Hoffman."

"Frederick Joseph Hoffmann."

"Michele L. Hoffmann."

"Judith Florence Hofmiller."

"Thomas Warren Hohlweck Jr."

"Jonathan R. Hohmann."

"Cora Hidalgo Holland."

"John Holland."

"Joseph F. Holland."

It was Kelly, who that day read the name of Joseph Holland, a Carr employee from Inwood who died on the same floor as Andrea. Later on, Gordy tracked down the man who read Andrea's name, and it turned out to be Joe Holland's brother. He'd read the name "Andrea Lyn Haberman," while Gordy and Ray Kelly had read a total of 28 others.

"Elizabeth Holmes."

"Thomas Holohan."

"Herbert Wilson Homer."

"Bradley Hoorn."

"James P. Hopper."

"Montgomery McCullough Hord."

"Michael Horn."

"Matthew Douglas Horning."

"Each one," says Gordy, "a life."

Chapter Thirty-four

Gordy didn't take many pictures that first time he was in New York in the days immediately following Sept. 11. In the summer of 2011, though, he got up off the bench in front of the Amish Market, took out his camera and started snapping shots of the city that was being renewed, and of the people who could be both unusually brusque and, in the aftermath of 9/11, uniquely empathetic. There is a part of Gordy, a big part, which only New Yorkers who also lost loved ones at the site can really empathize with, or know. And yet, ground zero is no longer where he envisions Andrea or where he himself feels best understood.

Gordy took a few more pictures, looked like a tourist for just a moment, and then walked north to catch the A train, which leads to the neighborhood known as Inwood at the northernmost tip of Manhattan. He got on the train and watched the stations roll by that morning, immersed in alternating shadows and light as he rode through the dark tunnels to the lighted platforms and back again. People came and went on the train. Most of the other passengers were too consumed in their own lives to listen to any part of his fascinating, heartrending story.

"You talk about tipping points in life and seminal moments and so on," said Gordy as the train sped north past the subway stops of Manhattan toward its last stop. Sept. 11 "certainly, certainly was it, and it wasn't a positive. But from that point on, after the initial month, month and a half, our associations continued to grow and to grow and to grow. Just when we seemed at our worst, we would hear something that would give us hope or to give us reaffirmation that Americans are generally good people, and positive people, despite the horrors that we saw — and it was horrific."

Gordy became convinced that Americans have a faith, hope and confidence in the future – as well as a compassion for those in need – that sets it apart from apart from much of the rest of the world.

Some of their post-9/11 associations, to be sure, were in Wisconsin — people like Maggie Gustafson, who helped found the Milwaukee chapter of Parents of Murdered Children. One of the best things Gordy and Kathy ever did back home was to reach out to her. Just talking to Maggie on the phone brought Kathy a little peace. They looked forward to Parents of Murdered Children meetings almost the way a young child would look forward to unwrapping a present — yet with a concurrent heaviness of heart that one wouldn't think could co-exist.

"We looked forward to it," said Gordy. "It helped us."

"We couldn't wait," added Kathy.

"We realized," said Gordy, "we are not alone."

Maggie remembers going to her first POMC meeting in Madison after her son Tony was killed in Milwaukee in 1995. He, like Andrea, was a completely innocent victim who just happened to be in the wrong place at the wrong time.

That first meeting was "probably the saddest thing I have ever been to, next to my son's funeral," said Maggie. "It was very sad because they go around this table and explain who they are and how their children died. The positive was that you saw that you were not always going to be feeling as bad as you did at that point." People sat there and functioned, then got up at the end and lived in the world. Everyone, it would turn out, does that in a slightly different way.

"There are no rules for grief," said Maggie. People mourn differently, process things differently, face different hurdles; come through it differently.

"Some people go on well and some don't. Everybody is different," she said.

One of the hurdles the Habermans and Al have always faced that she never had to, said Maggie, was being a 9/11 family.

"You have a child who died on 9/11, it makes you someone well-known in the community. And it's not something you really want to be known for," she said. It also meant that they could never really control reminders of it. Sept. 11 was a seminal event in American history, a national trauma that no one, especially many of the families, can ever fully get away from. The fact that the murder of a child remains inside you every day has a reflection in the outside world for the Sept. 11 families. There are constant reminders on TV, on the radio, in books and songs, and in passing comments overheard on a subway, a bus or a train.

"It is never going to go away. It will always be there," said Maggie. "They will be in the history books, for crying out loud." That is not easy, because references and reminders are sometimes what she calls "land mines." "They," she said of the Habermans, "have a lot of land mines."

Each member of the family has dealt with them differently. Kathy used to pretend that Andrea was just on a really long vacation. She wondered in the beginning if there would ever really be a future, and learned not to look toward one.

"I've learned to live for today and only for today because tomorrow might not come," she said. "I don't want any more disappointments."

She did eventually find solace, though, and it was always through faith.

"God will hold your hand and not let go," she said.

That does not mean there is ever real closure.

"Honestly," said Kathy in 2008, "I can say (time), maybe, has taught me to come in touch with my feelings better. Does it heal? No. ... You see all her friends getting married and having kids. Here's Al ... I hope he gets married and has a family. I want nothing else for him than to have that."

For Julie, she wishes the same thing. Kathy and Gordy's love for Julie is tangible, and they realize the burdens placed on her. One of the things Gordy worries about is the burden placed on Julie for the future — the burden of carrying the memories and the legacy of Sept. 11 in the years to come. It is one of the reasons he arranged to have Andrea's purse placed at the 9/11 Museum in New York. He doesn't want Julie to have to haul it around. It is one of the reasons, similarly, he wanted the story of Sept. 11 and of Andrea told in a book that can be read by future generations but also be put aside on a shelf and just be there, not always opened.

Asked in 2008 if life has unwound differently as a result of Sept. 11, Julie sat at her own table in her own home and answered.

"Unwound differently, and unwound," she said.

"It's hard for me to be OK with being happy," she said, reaching out and touching her boyfriend, Troy. "This, right here, is happiness."

A couple years after that, the happiness had blossomed into plans to get married in the spring of 2012. Father Haines, who had since been transferred to the Cathedral of St. John in downtown Milwaukee, had agreed to say the wedding. Thirty-two years old at the time, Julie said she and Troy planned to have a family. She smiled as she said it. Almost the only other thing that seems to bring as much happiness to her face as Troy is her discussion of dimes.

Julie has found many of them over the years in all sorts of circumstances.

Andrea liked to shop and, after she died, Julie received some of her clothes. One day, she said, she put her hand into the pocket of a brand-new pair of Andrea's pants, which still had the tag on them, and found a dime. Another time, Troy opened up the laundry chute to find a dime resting on the little ledge at the front that was no wider than a dime itself. Think about the physics of that, he said.

The most startling find, however, occurred on Andrea's birthday in 2008. Julie had been out to dinner that night with Nicole, Andrea's friend from high school. After Nicole had gone home, Julie was in the house alone, around 10 p.m., talking to her aunt Shelley on the phone. Troy and Julie had moved into the house less than two weeks earlier, and Julie had spent much of the day giving it an extremely thorough cleaning, even vacuuming the couch and going through boxes, while simultaneously baking a cake for Andrea's birthday. Julie had listened to her iPod Shuffle as she cleaned and baked.

Andrea had eclectic tastes in music, liked everything from grunge to the Beach Boys, and Julie remembers that her sister's favorite songs kept coming on. That night, Julie set a place for Andrea, cut her a piece of cake and poured her sister a glass of wine for her birthday, as if she were coming to dinner. She set it all on a placemat on a small table, lit some candles and placed a picture of Andrea there as well. Finally, she called Shelley and, sitting on a couch in the sunroom, she reminisced a little with her aunt.

Shelley asked Julie if she'd had a sign that day.

"No," responded Julie, "no sign. Nothing today or anything like that."

Until just then.

After their conversation, Julie hung up, carried the phone back into the kitchen, then returned to the couch she had vacuumed earlier in the day and where she had just sat as she talked with Shelley.

Right there "in the middle of the couch, where I was just sitting on the middle, were two dimes, side by side," she said. Julie appears jubilant when she talks about finding the 10-cent pieces. "Yeah," she said, sitting in her home not far from where she'd put out the cake and wine for her big sister and had found the dimes, "because I know she's listening. I know she is."

Julie has kept the dimes and a few more of Andrea's things that she cherishes most, but she eventually gave away many of her sister's belongings, such as clothes and household goods. "It was too much of a weight," she said. She had to make room for other things. She is more like her mom than her dad, in a key way. In the end, God and faith became her solace, too.

"He gets you through. He pulls you through. Shows you things you don't see. He opens your eyes. But you have to ask," said Julie in the summer of 2011. "I have always had faith and was raised Catholic, but I never knew what it meant to give it over to God. You have to go through all the crap to get to the other side."

"Andy is teaching me not to take life for granted; to know we don't get those days back, so make them count, and don't waste another day in anger and grief. I am with Jesus. I am exactly where I am supposed to be. It is almost like I can hear her say, 'What are you waiting for? Go for it! Go!' ... So, in a big way, I celebrate Andrea's life by moving ahead and enjoying my own. That is what she would have done in her own life. I know she is happy for Troy and me, and wants us to enjoy every second we have together building our life."

Kathy got her wish for Al as well. By the summer of 2011, Al, who had tuned 34 by then, had married and moved to Naperville, Ill. He still got back to the old neighborhood where he and Andrea had lived, still owned and rented out their old house and still bowled in the basement of a local Catholic church. Sipping a beer there late one Saturday night in the spring of 2011, he said he was on board with the telling of the 10 years since the Sept. 11 attacks. His more specific comments, though, were made a couple years earlier.

"Nothing positive came out of (9/11)," he said back then, standing in the house he had lived in with Andrea. "If something did, I can't think of it right now. ... But I'm not bitter and I'm not hateful."

He was, he said, able to enjoy life, although moving ahead had clearly been a gradual process. For the first few weeks after the attacks, he said, he hadn't been able to sleep in their bed. For the first year, he said, "I was real careful about not moving anything in the house that was hers. I wanted everything to stay where it was to the point where the garbage can upstairs had all of her stuff in it with tags."

He kept some personal things of Andrea's, such as jewelry he had given her. Eventually, though, he decided to renovate the house and try to sell it, so the bigger things of Andrea's had to be moved or donated.

For all he's been through, Al said that he doesn't think their story is the saddest.

"We didn't have any kids or anything like that," he said. "I couldn't imagine having three kids running around without their mom. I guess, in some respects, it's not that bad."

He's different than Gordy and Kathy in the end. He never felt attached to New York, never liked it. His solace came from his friends and family and coworkers over the years, and from his boss. In the early days, the paychecks never stopped coming. The donations to a scholarship fund at St. Norbert were always generous. Friends were "terrific."

Al, Julie, Gordy and Kathy had all followed slightly different paths by the summer of 2011, not long before the 10th anniversary of the attacks, when the A train Gordy was aboard slowed down and prepared to stop at Inwood. Gordy, at that time, was still waiting for the trials of Khalid Sheikh Mohammed and his four co-conspirators, hoped they would take place soon thereafter at the U.S. military base at Guantanamo Bay. Gitmo was still a distant stop on Gordy's journey and one he firmly believed would "make a difference" for him — but not the only one.

Gordy's journey was never just about justice. It was about Andrea, and trying to find a way to come to terms with the fundamental question of how she died in a place so far from home, separated from the people she loved.

The last stop that morning in the summer of 2011 was Inwood. Gordy, the last guy off the train, walked up the stairs out of the subway and made his way to the Church of the Good Shepherd — and to his answer.

Chapter Thirty-five

The Church of the Good Shepherd sits on Isham Street, which is also known as Inwood's Heroes of 9/11 Way.

The first thing you notice, walking from the A Train toward the church is the enormous, 20-foot-tall cross that, like the one Gordy pointed out down on Church Street near ground zero, had stood amid the ruins of the World Trade Center after the attacks. The Port Authority Police Department gave the cross to Good Shepherd in recognition of all the Inwood residents who were killed that day, many of whom were parishioners or who had once attended the church's grade school. Many of those residents grew up to be cops and firefighters who died trying to save the lives of others, and Gordy has come to believe they were not the only ones with that heroic inclination.

Just up the way from the cross is a garden that, in the spring spouts tulips and in the summer is redolent with brightly colored impatiens and hydrangea bushes that blossom beside evergreens inside a wrought-iron fence. A stone path leads past 23 markers that resemble gravestones, each with a name upon it, most of them Irish, one clearly German.

"Yeah, Donald McIntyre, Port Authority police officer," said Mike Meehan, walking slowly amid the stones with pictures of the deceased on them, pausing at one after another. "I went to kindergarten with this guy. We were in the same kindergarten class. ... a longtime friend of mine.

"Just a good guy, regular guy. He was in Jersey that morning ... and got called over to the World Trade Center. He was in there and doing his thing and helping people out; trying to get people out ... "

"Joe Holland," said Mike, motioning toward another stone of the Inwood man and Carr employee whose name was read in 2002 by Ray Kelly.

"Brendan Dolan," he said, nodding toward another stone. "One of the bosses at Carr Futures."

The list of the dead, "the boys" from the neighborhood as they are sometimes referred to, goes on. John Burnside, Tommy Dowd, Joe Kellett, Joe Leavey, and Damian Meehan — Mike's little brother and a guy who was likely sitting near Brendan Dolan and not all that far from Andrea when the plane hit the north tower. Each one, as Gordy would say, a story. Each one a life. Damian's life, said Mike, began in Inwood. He grew up on W. 207th St., now known as Damian Meehan Way. He played basketball and, of course, Gaelic football; married his wife, Joann, in June of 1998, and started a family.

Because they recovered Damian's body, said Mike, they knew he was in a stairwell with some firefighters and was apparently making his way down when the tower fell. He, in other words, had good reason for hope. Mike thinks that his little brother, having found a way out, had possibly stopped on the way down to give the firefighters a hand.

"Yeah, no problem," Mike envisions his little brother saying.

"These were strong guys," said Gordy. "If they could have made it out of there, they would have." It is a great comfort to him that "these were not passive individuals" nor self-centered ones. Gordy has learned that from and through their families.

"Mike knew our angst when we first met him," said Gordy. "We're from West Bend, Wisconsin. Andrea didn't know anybody. She had been in town for eight hours. Who was there to talk to?" Who was there to help her? To give her hope?

"They had broken through," said Gordy. "They ran out of time. But she would have been with them. ... They would have put their arms around her. They wouldn't have left her."

"She wasn't alone," added Mike. "You know what I'm saying? She wasn't alone. She was there with those guys ... She was one of the guys if you want to say it that way. But, you know, the thing with my brother and how that happened, I can't explain it just because of where he was recovered ... You know, so three weeks later we get him intact, and then a lot of the other workers from Carr Futures, some have never been recovered. Or just small pieces recovered ... I'm sure if he got down, he was getting other people down. You know, behind him."

Gordy is at peace, has a visible calmness about him, when he is out in Inwood at the memorial garden. To understand it, you must understand his greatest fear from the very beginning, from that morning when he woke up, stared in disbelief at towers aflame on TV and threw his coffee at the wall, was that his little girl was dying all alone amid strangers in a place she didn't know. Inwood is where that fear dissipates, where he knows the only truth that settles him, and where the ultimate question that he struggled with from the beginning is turned on its head. The question for Gordy in Inwood is no longer what the chances are somebody that would have helped and comforted Andrea that morning, and given her hope until the very last. The question now is: "What the chances that somebody would not have?" What really are the chances, the odds, that guys like Damian Meehan would not have helped and given hope?

"There is no doubt in my mind that Damian especially would have grabbed her," said Tricia Perrine, who knew Damian well. "Especially since she was sitting by the Energy Desk (where he worked). He would have taken her under his wing.

"They were such a family. In my mind, I picture them all together helping each other out."

In the end, there is no way to know for sure what happened in the final hour, of course, and all Gordy really knows about Damian Meehan or any of the others who died that morning is what he has seen of their families — and that is much of the point.

Gordy has witnessed some surprisingly mean-spirited people in the aftermath of that day: the Ward Churchills of the world, those who would mock the victims of murder. What never did get publicity and attention over the years were all the other people who impacted the lives of Gordy, Kathy, Julie and Al in very real ways: people like Jessica Kraemer, a girl who had the audacity of spirit to start searching for someone she had never even known; like Charlie Vitchers, who made a promise to recover Andrea that even he wasn't sure he could keep; like JoEllen Wichman, who knew that the meaning of the cross that she got from Cheerio Man was shared suffering — something Maggie Gustafson, who started the Parents of Murdered Children group in Milwaukee and helped the Habermans immensely, knew a little bit about as well. If Gordy and Kathy had faith, in the end, in the strength and goodness of people like Damian Meehan, it was also because of what they had come to know of others, such as Mike.

"My brother was me and then some, OK?" said Mike. "My brother was a great kid, great guy, well loved, well liked by all, and just a happy-go-lucky guy. I would say that that's some of the things (Gordy) sees, absolutely. Does he get comfort in that? Absolutely."

It is stunning how many Inwood boys died on the morning of Sept. 11, 2001, many of them from Good Shepherd. Anyone who doesn't think a war started that morning has never been to Inwood. If many parts of America never really felt the impact of those attacks personally, Inwood more than made up for it. There are some two dozen memorial stones in Good Shepherd's garden, and all commemorate kids who, at one time, ran in the neighborhood.

Almost all, that is.

Not far from Damian Meehan's stone, just across the path, is one for Andrea.

Andrea never set foot in Inwood when she lived. She had just made it to New York for the first time in her life the night before she was killed. So the connection to someone who does not know the story appears tenuous. To Gordy and Mike, it is anything but. It was Mike who asked others on a committee at Good Shepherd if Andrea could be included in the garden.

"You know (the Habermans) have no affiliation with New York other than, unfortunately, Andrea passing here on 9/11," said Mike. "And I felt that they should have a home here in New York, and why not be in the memorial garden?"

"Listen," he said to Gordy at the time, "we have a garden up here. I'm going to bring it to the committee. I would really love it if you and your family would be a part of New York, part of Inwood. And I'm going to propose that Andrea's stone be placed here, along with all the great men that we lost."

Gordy, who rarely gets emotional, succumbs when he talks about Andrea being included in the garden, and about the gesture that Mike made and the rest of the committee voted to support. Folks could easily have opposed it or secretly lobbied against it, after all, because this is Inwood's garden and these are Inwood's heroes. Why include a girl from Wisconsin, of all places? The memorial garden is about Inwood's family, which is precisely why it meant so much to Gordy and Kathy.

"You have to understand, Mike adopted our family. There is no other way to explain that. I get emotional about that, sorry," said Gordy.

"I'm not Catholic and I'm not Irish," he quipped. "Think about that."

When Gordy and Kathy are in New York now, they invariably go to Inwood. There is no physical part of Andrea, nor of any of the others, there. Damian, for instance, is buried in St. Anastasia Cemetery in Harriman, NY. But Good Shepherd is where his family is almost every day, where Damian's Irish mom walks out of Mass in the morning and stops to talk. The memorial garden, says Gordy, is where he feels Andrea's presence.

Sitting in a local restaurant in Inwood, Gordy mulled over a question about whether, absent Mike Meehan and Charlie Vitchers and others like them — people who brought Andrea and her memory back to him in a very real way — he would have become bitter.

"I think I could have barked up the wrong tree and become very disillusioned," he said. "I couldn't believe Andrea was here. There are no odds for her being here, and we refused to let that go. And so whatever was going to be out in New York, we were going to find out things. But fortunately, what happened to us is we met good people who cared about Andrea. Nobody here ever knew Andrea. There's no connection with Andrea whatsoever. The only thing they knew about Andrea is maybe what they've read, or through us."

There is still disbelief at times. It's impossible, as Gordy noted, to not at least occasionally think about the odds and the "what ifs." Fate's dice should never in a billion years have come up the way they did with Andrea. It makes one wonder if they were loaded. There were, as Gordy said, just no odds for her being in New York in the north tower on the 92nd floor on Sept. 11. And yet she was. That alone was something that took months, maybe even years, to digest. It really did happen. And if it could happen to Andrea, an innocent young woman from the Midwest, it could happen to anyone.

Yet, if it's human nature to equate simple bad luck with some sort of cosmic and   depressing stacking of the odds against both innocent victims and the hope of a basically beneficent world, surely there is a more sanguine flipside, too. Some of the "God links" that manifested themselves over the years were so odds-defying in themselves that there was a commensurate impulse to see something greater and more meaningful there as well. What are the odds of Andrea peering up from the Reader's Digest at just the right time? Of finding a dime in a shoebox in New York or on a couch back in Wisconsin on Andrea's birthday? Indeed, of Scott coming into Gordy's life at just the right time and Gordy's going into Scott's? Of Jessica Kraemer?

There is no scale that measures out and weighs all the good stuff and all the bad stuff in the world, good on one side, evil on the other, or even faith on the left and knowledge on the right. Things are much messier than that. Sometimes hope and despair are intertwined, as are faith in the goodness of most people's hearts and knowledge of the horrors that, if dwelt upon too steadfastly, would leave anyone bitter.

Gordy wrote as much way back in 2002, in a remembrance of Andrea that Tricia Perrine included in the book she put together to memorialize the 69 Carr employees killed on Sept. 11 in the north tower. Gordy and Kathy had started meeting with some of the other Carr families at the time, getting to know the families and learning more about how their loved ones had died. It was bittersweet.

Sweet, suggested Gordy, in that "as we sat and shared portions of our loved ones' lives and indeed their last moments, Kathy and I came away with some sense of peace that many good and loved people were with her that day. ... We came away with an understanding that Andrea would have been held and hugged and protected as best possible in a situation such as this."

Bitter though, too, because "from this meeting, we also confirmed what we had all feared: that, if possible, the events of that terrible day were more horrific for the people on the 92nd floor. They suffered longer. They were trapped, tortured and then murdered; hopefully, before being mutilated. This will never be erased from any of our minds. All of them deserved more from life than what they received. It is amazing to Kathy and I that any of us can talk of that day."

They do, though, Gordy especially.

He talks of it unflinchingly and in a way that really can be surprisingly blunt, and courageous. For years he has courageously asked every question he could think of regarding what happened to Andrea and why, and did so knowing full well that the answers would be disturbing. He did it for Andrea and for the rest of his family and for himself, as the last act of a father whose whole mission and purpose in life was protecting his girls. He has never turned away from the answers. He has endured them no matter the pain or the cost. He has not, however, endured them alone. He has benefitted greatly from the empathy of people such as Charlie Vitchers, who realized he could easily have been Gordy, and of Mike Meehan, who lost a brother.

"They," says Gordy of the New Yorkers, "know loss."

"They know what it is," is how Kathy puts it. "Almost everybody in New York had a friend or a loved one that had died or worked there, so there's no explaining that has to be done."

There is a big caveat to all the relationships in New York: Kathy and Gordy would, of course, rather have Andrea back than any of those friends that mean so much to them. "But the friends that we've met, I feel that they've given me so much courage and strength and faith, restored that in myself, that I can be a human being again," said Kathy.

Gordy and Kathy go to Inwood often, but it was Kathy's words at a dedication of Andrea's memorial in September of 2006 that resonated most deeply. Kathy arranged for the release of 40 doves in the garden that morning. As they flew upward she said a prayer for grace and strength.

"You are forever present in our hearts and souls," she said. "May we find the inner peace we long for, knowing we will be reunited."

As for Gordy, his quest will not be over until the trials at Guantanamo, if then. He is a and fact finder, and yet, as he discovered at ground zero, facts only take one so far before you have to make a leap toward something to believe in and take home with you at the end of the journey.

Chapter Thirty-six

In the spring of 2005, shortly after they found out about the "pause" at the medical examiner's office, Gordy arranged for Andrea's remains to be sent to a crematory in Chester, New York. The crematory, in turn, sent them to the McManus & Ahern Funeral Home on W. 43rd St., where the ashes were placed in a white, cardboard box with a handle on it. On the box was a "certificate of cremation" stating that "Andrea Lyn Haberman has been cremated at Oxford Hills Crematory, Inc." on March 26, 2005. The Habermans could have arranged to have the funeral home in New York City send the box back to Wisconsin. There are formal processes and procedures set up for that sort of thing. They felt, however, that Andrea deserved more. They wanted to fly out and pick the box up themselves.

"She is not coming home alone," is the way Gordy put it.

He, Kathy and Julie made the trip out to New York. They picked up the box at the funeral home and walked out, proceeding somberly down a street in Manhattan.

"Had her in a box," said Gordy. "A plastic bag inside."

As they walked along, Gordy handed the box to Julie, who would later call it the "heaviest tiny box" she had ever felt.

As they walked along, a woman in front of them fell off the curb and hurt herself rather badly. She was bleeding and needed help, but no one was stopping to assist her. People were just walking right past. So the Habermans stopped, helped the woman off the street and into the shade and tried to apply a little pressure to her wound. They asked someone to call the police and then stayed with the woman and waited for the police to show up. After the police came and took over, they took the box, walked down the block and across the street and got a booth at a restaurant. They asked that an extra place be set at the table for lunch.

The next morning at ground zero, Al joined them at a private Mass in the Port Authority family room overlooking the pit. Father Brian Jordan, a Franciscan priest who prayed twice a day in front of the cross that would later be moved to the National September 11 Memorial and Museum, said the funeral service. It was just the opposite of the huge memorial gathering in late September of 2001 back in West Bend. This time, there were no crowds and no reporters, no doubt either about where Andrea was or what had happened to her. They grieved in private before taking the ashes in the cardboard box onto a plane and carrying her home. Gordy, who had bought two different containers, divided up the ashes at the airport in Milwaukee, gave some to Al and kept the rest. Then, they took Andrea's ashes the final leg of the journey back to Farmington.

Jack Philips, a West Bend mortician who had coordinated the memorial service at no cost, has a workshop at his farm, Gordy said one afternoon in August 2011. Jack and some members of his family made a beautiful wooden box with a cross inlaid in the top, he recalled, and gave the gift to the Habermans. They put Andrea's ashes in the box and placed it in the living room of their home, beneath purple orchids. Purple is the color of suffering, but it was also Andrea's favorite.

The box sits on a table in the back of the house near windows that look out upon the backyard where the pictures had been taken the day after Andrea and Al became engaged. So part of Andrea, the physical part, is perhaps still in the dust of ground zero along with so many other unidentified remains, part is in Illinois, and part is in Wisconsin, in the box with the cross inlaid into the top. Andrea's presence is felt in all those places and in Inwood, and, at times, in spots were dimes turn up unexpectedly and poems are read. Beside the box is a laminated copy of the Henry Scott Holland poem that showed up next to a picture of Andrea in Reader's Digest, "Death is nothing at all."

"I have only slipped away into the next room," it begins. "I am I, and you are you. Whatever we were to each other, that we are still."

Nearby as well is the cross that Cheerio Man gave to JoEllen and that JoEllen, after having it divided, gave to Gordy and Kathy. And beside that is the cross that Charlie Vitchers gave to them that first day they met him in April of 2002 at ground zero when he made his promise to find Andrea. Both crosses – as well as a Gaelic cross the Meehans gave the Habermans and that Gordy keeps in his office – are a reminder of friendship and faith and something Father Haines tried to impress on them over the years. Regardless of what happened on that last morning, Andrea was never alone.

"You couldn't be there physically," he wanted them to know, "but you were there spiritually by teaching these girls from the get-go as little children that God was with them."

They, when all was said and done in the end, were with her as well.

"We weren't able to be with her at the time of her death," said Gordy. "But we came home as a family again."

In the end, that is what Gordy, Kathy, Julie and Al focus on the most, family — and what it means to be one. The loss of Andrea, like the tragedy of Sept. 11 itself, reverberated through their families and communities for years; still did in the late summer of 2011 as the 10th anniversary approached. There can never be a counterweight to their loss, but there were other reverberations as well: countless good and generous things, gestures of love and support, "compassion given freely," to borrow one of Gordy's phrases, that provided a way through the grief and sadness. It was Kathy's sister Terry who articulated how friends reached out and helped in ways big and small, some just bringing food, others donating money or letting dogs out, others doing bigger things for Gordy, Kathy, Julie and Al that would help them through.

"If you are strong enough and determined enough to look through the pain, these little rays of the power of the human spirit are there," she said. "You just have to be willing to look. I don't mean that from a Pollyannaish perspective. But if you keep them in mind, they are there for you" when they are needed most.

Henry Scott Holland was wrong about one thing in his poem. Life, at least for the family members of Sept. 11 victims, is not the same as it ever was.

"You have all these plans and projections for your life, and in one hour it is trashed. You are constantly behind this wall and you can't get over it or around it. You can only confront it on a daily basis," said Gordy, sitting not far from the ashes of his daughter in early August 2011.

"The best laid plans of mice and men often go astray."

What occurred was simply and literally beyond imagining.

"I never thought ever that one of my daughters would die so horrifically," said Kathy. It is still difficult at times, she said, not to imagine the "what ifs" because Andrea was on the cusp of so much that never happened in the 10 years since 2001. And yet, they look, too, at what has happened.

"We could not talk about this unless the grief was balanced with good, the evil balanced with the good," Gordy said.

While they have learned that the future is an unpredictable thing, they have also learned that there is much more to life than the grief and sorrow of the past. There is the present.

That very morning, said Kathy, in fact, Julie had called and said that her wedding dress had come in; asked Kathy to go and look at it with her.

"It is beautiful," said Kathy, and Julie looked beautiful in it.

"I could tell she was looking to the future and what life has in store for her," said Kathy. "I had the biggest smile on my face. Life does go on and we have a lot to live for.

"Today was an exceptional day."

Acknowledgements

I long ago lost track of the number of times I interviewed Gordy for this book, surely dozens — and that isn't even counting the hundreds of emails and quick, five-minute conversations on the phone. I am indebted to him for his time, his research, his knowledge, but mostly for his trust. Thank you, Gordy, for trusting me with your story, and with Andrea's memory. My one regret in this whole project is that I never knew her.

Kathy, Julie and Al were generous with their help, their honesty and their support — as were countless members of extended families and friends who allowed me into their homes and their lives.

Books are time-consuming endeavors. No one knows this better than Jane, my wife and ever-supportive best friend. Jane pulled weeds in the yard, ferried the kids and did her own full-time job while I sat in the attic and wrote. She was also, along with my friends Dave Umhoefer and Sheri Bestor, an invaluable editor who gave me ample amounts of time and comment on short notice. John Haines, the author of a fine book called *Danny Mo*, generously shared his many secrets. He led me to Paul Slotty, Justen Preiss and R. Christopher Cain, the crew at P.S. Finishing Inc. who provided formatting, cover work and guidance. Thanks must also go to Louann Schoenberg, for her fine copy editing under deadline pressure, and to my mom, Mary Nichols, who still has her English teacher's eye; to Drew Wandschneider for his inspired cover art, Erinn Vogel for her assistance, and Charlie Sykes for early reading and help. To Marty Kaiser, the editor of the Milwaukee Journal Sentinel, for his interest and support, thank you. This book is a very good thing. All of you helped make it so.

ABOUT THE AUTHOR

Mike Nichols is an award-winning, syndicated newspaper columnist and senior fellow at the Wisconsin Policy Research Institute.

In addition to *Just a Few Sleeps Away*, he is also the author of *The Waking*, a mystery published by HarperCollins.

A graduate of Boston College and the University of Chicago, he lives in Cedarburg, Wis., with his wife, Jane, and their three kids. He can be reached at MRNichols@wi.rr.com .

CPSIA information can be obtained at www.ICGtesting.com
Printed in the USA
LVOW011932100911

245719LV00006B/10/P